Cambridge
First Certificate
in English
3

TEACHER'S BOOK

Examination papers from the
University of Cambridge
Local Examinations Syndicate

CAMBRIDGE
UNIVERSITY PRESS

PUBLISHED BY THE PRESS SYNDICATE OF THE UNIVERSITY OF CAMBRIDGE
The Pitt Building, Trumpington Street, Cambridge CB2 1RP, United Kingdom

CAMBRIDGE UNIVERSITY PRESS
The Edinburgh Building, Cambridge CB2 2RU, United Kingdom
40 West 20th Street, New York, NY 10011–4211, USA
10 Stamford Road, Oakleigh, Melbourne 3166, Australia

First published 1997
Third printing 1998

Printed in the United Kingdom at the University Press, Cambridge

ISBN 0 521 58726 3 Student's Book
ISBN 0 521 58725 5 Teacher's Book
ISBN 0 521 58724 7 Set of 2 Cassettes

Contents

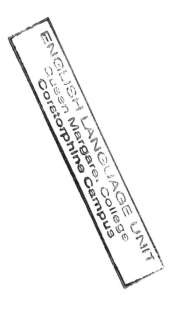

Introduction

The level of FCE

The First Certificate in English (FCE) offers an intermediate-level qualification for those wishing to use English for professional or study purposes. In order to take into account developments in language teaching and testing, the FCE examination was revised in December 1996.

FCE candidates

In 1996 there were approximately 250,000 candidates for FCE throughout the world. Candidates come from a wide range of backgrounds and take the examination for a number of different reasons. The following points summarise the characteristics of the current FCE candidature.

Nationality

FCE is taken by candidates throughout the world in about 100 countries, although the total number of nationalities represented in the candidature is over 150. The majority of these candidates enter for FCE in European and South American countries.

Age and gender

Most candidates (about 75%) are under 25, with the average age being about 22. In some countries the average age is lower (e.g. in Greece it is about 17 years old). About 65% of candidates are female.

Employment

Most candidates are students, although there are considerable differences in the proportion of students in different countries.

Exam preparation

A large proportion of candidates (about 80%) undertake a preparatory course before taking the examination; most of these courses last between eight and 24 weeks.

Reasons for taking FCE

Candidates' reasons for wanting an English language qualification are roughly distributed as follows:

- to gain employment (37%)
- for further study (30%)
- out of personal interest (33%)

The structure of FCE: *an overview*

UCLES (University of Cambridge Local Examinations Syndicate) has developed a series of examinations with similar characteristics spanning five levels. Within the series of five levels, the First Certificate in English is at Cambridge Level Three:

Cambridge Level 5 Certificate of Proficiency in English (CPE)
Cambridge Level 4 Certificate in Advanced English (CAE)
Cambridge Level 3 First Certificate in English (FCE)
Cambridge Level 2 Preliminary English Test (PET)
Cambridge Level 1 Key English Test (KET)

The FCE examination consists of five papers:

Paper 1	**Reading**	1 hour 15 minutes
Paper 2	**Writing**	1 hour 30 minutes
Paper 3	**Use of English**	1 hour 15 minutes
Paper 4	Listening	40 minutes (approximately)
Paper 5	Speaking	14 minutes (approximately)

Paper 1 Reading

Candidates are expected to be able to read semi-authentic texts of various kinds (informative and general interest) and to show understanding of gist, detail and text structure, and to deduce meaning.

The paper contains four parts. Each part contains a text and corresponding comprehension tasks. One part may contain two or more shorter related texts.

Paper 2   Writing

Candidates are expected to be able to write non-specialised text types such as letters, articles, reports and compositions for a given purpose and target reader, covering a range of topics. One of the tasks in Part 2 is based on an optional reading of one of five set books.

Candidates are required to carry out two tasks: a compulsory task in Part 1 and one task from a choice of four in Part 2. The overall word length of answers across the two tasks is 240–360 words.

Paper 3   Use of English

Candidates are expected to demonstrate their knowledge and control of the language system by completing a number of tasks, some of which are based on specially written texts.

The paper contains five parts and 65 questions, which take the form of multiple-choice cloze, open cloze, 'key' word transformations, error correction and word formation task types.

Paper 4   Listening

Candidates are provided with short extracts and longer monologues, announcements, extracts from radio programmes, news, features, etc., at an intermediate level. They are expected to show understanding of detail and gist, and to deduce meaning.

The paper contains four parts. Each part contains a recorded text or texts and corresponding comprehension tasks.

Paper 5   Speaking

Candidates are examined in pairs by two examiners, one acting as **Interlocutor** and the other as **Assessor**. The four parts of the test are based on verbal prompts and visual stimuli and are designed to elicit a wide range of speaking skills and strategies from both candidates.

Accuracy of grammar and appropriacy of vocabulary, discourse management, pronunciation and interactive communication are assessed.

Marks

Each of the papers carries 40 marks after weighting.

Further information

FCE is held each year in June and December in 1,900 centres worldwide. Special arrangements are available for disabled candidates. These may include extra time, separate accommodation or equipment, Braille transcription, etc. Consult the UCLES Local Secretary in your area for more details.

Copies of the Regulations and details of entry procedure, current fees and further information about this and other Cambridge examinations can be obtained from the Local Secretary for UCLES examinations in your area, or from:

Administration and Systems Division
UCLES
1 Hills Road
Cambridge
CB1 2EU
Telephone: +44 1223 553311
Fax: +44 1223 460278

In some areas this information can also be obtained from the British Council.

FCE content and marking

Paper 1   Reading

The FCE Reading paper contains four parts. Each part consists of a text and corresponding comprehension tasks. One part may contain two or more shorter related texts. There is a total of 35 questions. The time allowed to select answers and record them on the answer sheet is one hour fifteen minutes.

Texts

The length of FCE texts varies from 350 words to 700 words, depending on the type of task. The total reading load for the paper is approximately 1,900 to 2,300 words. The texts are intended to cover a range of recently published material and to appear authentic in form, presentation and content.

Texts may be of the following types:
- advertisements
- correspondence
- fiction
- information material (brochures, guides, manuals)
- messages
- newspaper/magazine articles
- reports

Pictures and other diagrams are used where appropriate to illustrate the text; questions do not focus on visual elements. Some of the vocabulary may be simplified in the texts to keep it within the FCE level but such changes are kept to a minimum.

Test focus

The tasks in the Reading paper test candidates' ability to:
- understand gist and main ideas
- understand detail
- follow text structure
- deduce meaning
- select specific information

Tasks

There are 35 questions on the Reading paper. Each text is accompanied by a set of questions as follows:

Part	Task	Number of Questions	Task Format
1	Multiple matching	6 or 7	Candidates must match a heading or summary sentence to paragraphs of the text.
2	Multiple choice	7 or 8	Candidates must answer multiple-choice questions based on the text.
3	Gapped text	6 or 7	Candidates must select appropriate paragraphs or sentences that have been removed from the text and jumbled.
4	Multiple matching	13–15	Candidates must locate relevant information in the text or texts.

Multiple-choice and gapped-text questions follow the text; multiple-matching questions precede the text.

The language level of the instructions and individual questions is within the range of FCE.

Marks

Candidates record their answers by shading the correct lozenges on a separate answer sheet.

Two marks are given for each correct answer in **Parts 1, 2** and **3** and one mark is given for each correct answer in **Part 4**. The total score is then weighted to 40 marks for the whole of the Reading paper.

Marking

The Reading paper is directly scanned by computer.

Paper 2 Writing

The FCE Writing paper requires candidates to carry out two tasks; a compulsory task in **Part 1** and one from a choice of four questions in **Part 2**. Candidates are expected to write 120–180 words for each task, making a total overall word length of 240–360 words across the two tasks. The time allowed to complete the two tasks is one hour thirty minutes. There is an optional question on background reading texts in **Part 2**.

Test focus

Part 1 is a compulsory task in which candidates have to produce a transactional letter. Information is given about a specific situation through a combination of text and notes, sometimes supported by illustrations or diagrams. In **Part 2** there is a choice of four tasks from which candidates choose one. All of the questions specify why the piece is to be written and who the piece is to be written for.

   Parts 1 and **2** carry equal marks.

Tasks

In **Part 1**, the language of the reading input and rubric is well within the level expected of FCE candidates. Candidates are required to write a transactional letter in an appropriate style. The purpose of the letter and the addressee is clearly explained in the rubric. In order to complete the task successfully, candidates need to use the input provided in an appropriate way, expanding on the points given by using a range of structures and vocabulary.

In **Part 2**, candidates are expected to write one of the following:

- an article
- an informal/non-transactional letter
- a discursive composition
- a descriptive/narrative composition/short story
- a report
- a letter of application

There is an optional task (question 5) on background reading texts in **Part 2**. There are two alternatives in question 5 and candidates may select one of these based on their reading of the set texts. The list of set texts is published by UCLES in the examination regulations. Each text normally remains on the list for two years.

Assessment

An impression mark is awarded to each task; examiners use band descriptors similar to the ones on page 8 to assess how well the task has been realised.

   The **general impression mark scheme** is used in conjunction with a **task-specific mark scheme**, which focuses on criteria specific to each particular task, including relevance, length, omissions, range of structure/vocabulary, layout and register.

   Allowances are made for appropriate colloquialisms and American usage and spelling; marks are not specifically deducted for spelling errors, although a number of errors which interfere with communication will affect the assessment.

GENERAL MARK SCHEME

5	Full realisation of task set shown by: • All content points included. • Wide range of structure and vocabulary within the task set. • Minimal errors, perhaps due to ambition; well-developed control of language. • Ideas effectively organised and paragraphed, with a variety of linking devices. • Register and format consistently appropriate to purpose and audience. Fully achieves the desired effect on the target reader.
4	Good realisation of the task set. • All major content points included: possibly one or two minor omissions. • Good range of structure and vocabulary within the task. • Generally accurate, errors occur mainly when attempting more complex language. • Ideas clearly organised and paragraphed, with suitable linking devices. • Register and format on the whole appropriate to purpose and audience. Achieves the desired effect on the target reader.
3	Reasonable achievement of the task set. • All major content points included; some minor omissions. • Adequate range of structure and vocabulary, which fulfils the requirements of the task. • A number of errors may be present, but they do not impede communication. • Ideas adequately organised and paragraphed, with simple linking devices. • Reasonable, if not always successful attempt at register and format appropriate to purpose and audience. Achieves, on the whole, the desired effect on the target reader.
2	Task set attempted but not adequately achieved. • Some major content points inadequately covered or omitted, and/or some irrelevant material. • Limited range of structure and vocabulary. • A number of errors, which distract the reader and may obscure communication at times. • Ideas inadequately organised and paragraphed; linking devices rarely used. • Unsuccessful/inconsistent attempts at appropriate register and format. Message not clearly communicated to target reader.
1	Poor attempt at task set. • Notable content omissions and/or considerable irrelevance, possibly due to misinterpretation of task set. • Narrow range of vocabulary and structure. • Frequent errors which obscure communication; little evidence of language control. • Lack of organisation, paragraph or linking devices. • Little or no awareness of appropriate register and format. Very negative effect on the target reader.
0	Achieves nothing: too little language for assessment (fewer than 50 words) or totally illegible.

All of these comments should be interpreted at FCE level, and referred to in conjunction with a task-specific mark scheme.

Marking

The panel of examiners is divided into small teams, each with a very experienced examiner as Team Leader. The Principal Examiner guides and monitors the marking process. This begins with a meeting of the Principal Examiner and the Team Leaders. This is held immediately after the examination and begins the process of establishing a common standard of assessment by the selection of sample scripts for all five questions in Paper 2. Sample scripts are chosen to demonstrate the range of responses and different levels of competence, and a **task-specific mark scheme** is finalised for each individual question on the paper. This summarises the **content, organisation, cohesion, range** of structures and vocabulary, **register, format** and **target reader** indicated in the tasks, in the form of satisfactory descriptors. The accuracy of language, including spelling and punctuation, is assessed on the general impression scale for all tasks. Markers discuss these individual mark schemes and refer to them regularly while they are working. A rigorous process of co-ordination and checking is carried out before and throughout the marking process.

Sample answers and examiner's comments

The following pieces of writing have been selected from students' answers produced during trialling. The samples relate to tasks in Tests 1–4 of the Student's Book. Explanatory notes have been added to show how the bands have been arrived at. The comments should be read in conjunction with the task-specific mark schemes included in the keys.

Sample A (Test 1, Question 2 – Report)

> *You will find all kinds of shop in the college's area. First of all, there is a big supermarkt at only five minutes walk from the students' residence. It is open from 9. a. m to 7. p. m well furnished and not too expensive.*
>
> *If you don't like cooking, you'll have a large choice of pubs and restaurants, where you can have a good meal and meet nice people. Some of them could be too expensive for students, so you have to be careful and to read previously the menue. The White Horse is the oldest pub in the Town. It is always crowded and very noisy, but it is worth going there if you want to meet local people.*
>
> *You'll also find several bookshops in the town's centre. The shop assistants are usually very competent and helpful. Last but not least, a doctor's surgery, a chemist and a bank are located in Browning Street, not far away from the main building of the campus.*

Comments

Information is given about different kinds of shops (supermarket, bookshops, chemist) and relevant details such as opening times have been included. There is some digression on pubs and restaurants, which has brought the mark down from a Band 4.

The writing flows naturally and there is evidence of range. Relevant student vocabulary such as *residence, campus* has been included.

The piece is well controlled, with occasional non-impeding errors, e.g. *to read previously the menue*. Appropriate paragraphing has been attempted although perhaps not distinctly enough for a report.

The register is generally appropriate.

The target reader would be well-informed.

Band: 3

Sample B (Test 1, Question 3 – Informal Letter)

Dear Susan,

How are you? I'm very well here in Rome. I'm here since the last week but I'm going to stay until the next week. Rome is precious, for me one of the most beautiful cities in the world.

    The museums and the archaeological excavations are magnificent. We have visited the Forum wich is all the monuments from the Roman period. The Coliseum near the Forum is beautiful and enormous (about 60.000 came here to see the lions vs christions fights), the Vatican city is beautiful. We saw the pope here in San Pedro. You will enjoy Rome because here the museums are very good. The Vatican museums are so big that we spend five hours for visiting it. The Borghese Gallery where the Apollo and Dague by Bernini is the Capitolium museum etc. Yesterday we went to S.Pietro in Vincoli, there is the Moses by Miguel Angel.

    Tomorrow we are going to the Piazza di Spaguna and to the Fontana de Trevi (where Anita Baker swim in the film "La Dolce Vita" by Fellinin.

    I will show you the photographs when I'll be back.

    Yours,

       Marianne

Comments

Plenty of detail is given on what the writer has done so far but there is very little about future plans and no reference to the group.

    There is evidence of range, with some good descriptive language used, e.g. … *the archaeological excavations are magnificent.* A number of non-impeding errors are present, e.g. *I'm here since the last week … The Vatican museums are so big that we spend five hours for visiting it.* At one point – *The Borghese Gallery …* – there is lack of control.

    The letter is well organised, with some paragraphing and a good opening.

    The register is consistently informal.

    The target reader would find the description interesting but expect a wider range of information.

Band: 2

Sample C (Test 1, Question 4 – Composition)

"*Violence in t.v. and on films can make young people behave badly.*"

Many people belive that such kind of T.V and films are bad for young people. I agree with that.

In my opinion is it is very easy to see such seans in there therefore they will be able to kow how to fight to other people and hurt to other people. However, the will not be able to know how it is hurt and dengerous is. It is so bad to grow up for young people that they might have alcohol and smoak, even though they are not grow up enough.

To sum up. they should not watch such kind of programs until they have common.

Comments

Although the writer states agreement early in the composition, inadequate reasons are given. The script is also rather short.

There is little evidence of FCE level language, apart from some vocabulary items, e.g. *grow up, alcohol.*

There is serious lack of control and the errors made are basic, frequent and often impeding. The final sentence exemplifies this. The piece has been paragraphed and there is some attempt to use cohesive devices.

The register is acceptable.

The target reader would be confused and might not read to the end.

Band: 1

Sample D (Test 2, Question 3 – Application)

Dear Mrs Robinson,

  I have read your advertisement in The Guardian Weekly's today issue and I am very interested in your job offer as a waitress I hope you will be interested in my application.

  First, I am a foreign student. French is my mother-tongue but I have also learnt English and German at school. Now I am learning English at the University to become a teacher in English for French pupils. My knowledge of French must be useful for you as the Eurostar attracks a lot of French visitors in Britain nowadays. As a student in English, I am both interested in earning money at summer time and in learning Britain and its inhabitants.

  Secondly, if I have no experience in working in a restaurant, I have already had a summer job in a shop. So, I am used to the wishes of customers, the concern in welcoming them clearly and the hurry in which you sometimes are. Then, I am 30 years old, that is old enough to understand choosy customers, but young enough to deal with hard work conditions and heavy schedules.

  To conclude, I am highly motivated to your job offer and free as soon as you need me. Looking forward to a positive answer,
  Your sincerely

  Betsy Prel

Comments

The points in the advertisement have been covered and the writer has submitted a strong application.

  There is evidence of structural range and complex sentences are produced successfully. Very good vocabulary is also used, e.g. *conditions, schedules*. A few non-impeding errors e.g. *a student in English, learning Britain.*

  Generally the letter is controlled and accurate; errors occur mainly when complex sentences are attempted, e.g. ... *the concern in welcoming* ...

  The letter is very well-organised and suitably paragraphed with an appropriate ending.

  The register is consistently formal.

  The target reader would consider the application seriously.

Band: 5

Sample E (Test 2, Question 4 – Short Story)

> Bernie woke suddenly and looked at the bed-side clock. It was three o'clock in the morning and he remembered it was his mother's birthday. So he thought to prepair a surprise and for when she woke up at nine o'clock everything must be ready. First of all he went to the kitchen to cook a chocolate cake, but he noticed there was no milk and it was imposible to do without it. So Bernie dressed up in silence and walked very slowly to the door. Obviously at that time in the morning everything was close and he thought in his friend Judith, she lived infront of his house but it was very early to knock to the door. So Bernie took some little stones and tryed to put them in her window. After a lot of time, Judith saw him and went to the door and gave him the milk. After that Bernie start doing every thing a little faster because there wasn't more time. He prepaired the cake and put a lot of balloons in all the house. At 8.30 he took a beautiful breakfast to his mother's room, everything was perfect, the cake had many candles on it and his mother was starting to wake up. Right on time!

Comments

The writer has used the prompt well and written an imaginative story with a good ending.

A straightforward narrative using mainly the simple past. Some good vocabulary relevant to the story has been introduced, e.g. *balloons, candles*. There are a number of errors in structure, e.g. *he thought to prepair, to put them in her window.* Spelling is also problematic, e.g. *prepair, imposible.*

The story follows a logical sequence and linking devices are used to good effect. The final phrase: *Right on time!* is effective. Some paragraphing would have improved the presentation, particularly as it is rather long.

The register is satisfactory.

The target reader would probably enjoy the story.

Band: 3

Sample F (Test 3, Question 1 – Formal Letter)

> Dear Brecon Boating Holidays
>
> We are 4 friends and we are interested in the cruise along the rivers and canals that you are advertising. There are some information that we want to know before making our reservations. First of all, we want to know how much it would cost us 1 week for four people. We also want to know how fast the boats travel and how far each day. Another thing that we think it is important is if we need to bring special clothes and if the cooking equipment is included or we also have to take it with us. Finally, we would like to know some more about loxury in your boats.
>
> We are very happy and we really want to take part of this great and interesting adventure Please send us the answers of our questions and all the informatin that you think it is important and necessary to know.
>
> Thank you,
>
> Rona Storck

Comments

All the points have been covered.

A variety of indirect question forms are attempted. The opening sentence shows evidence of control. Some relevant vocabulary is used, e.g. *reservations*. Although there are some errors, these do not impede the meaning, e.g. *There are some information … how much it would cost us 1 week for four people. … take part of.*

The letter is well-organised: the writer makes early reference to the advertisement and states her queries clearly, using linking devices.

The register is occasionally rather informal for a letter of this kind, e.g. *We are very happy …*

The target reader would be able to respond to the letter and deal with the questions raised.

Band: 4

Sample G (Test 4, Question 3 – Article)

Clothes and Personalities

Today, No one escape to the fashion. Even the ones that called themselves "alternatives" follow some "fashion" that belongs to them. We don't see people walking down the street wearing clothes from the '70s. We don't see either, 15 year old girls wearing clothes of people of 60 years old. We don't see people wearing scarf and gloves in summer. So, everyone follow the fashion: if distinguish us from other classes (middle class, low class, high class), from the other sex, from our parents, and from our sons. All these has an influence on our personalities: some people say that the way you dress reflect the way you are: Tidy, hard-working, if you care yourself, etc. Other people say that you dressed following the fashion, and you don't put your personal 'detail' on your cloth.

*   Maybe, this thing of seeing "through" the cloth is an ability. The truth is that with or without this "ability", the fashion dictated what you are going to put next.*

Comments

Although some attempt has been made at producing an article, the writer does not address the task adequately – a general description of trends is given, rather than own or friends' views. There is also very little on the link between clothes and personality.

There is some ambition, though this is marred by errors. Good vocabulary is used, e.g. *follow (the) fashion, distinguish, reflect, dictated*. However, these items are used inaccurately.

A high number of errors distract the reader. Communication is obscured at times, see e.g. sentence beginning *Maybe this thing of seeing …*

There is some attempt to organise the piece, with a strong opening sentence. Paragraphing is insufficient and the article ends abruptly.

The register is satisfactory and article format has been attempted, including a title.

The target reader would be rather confused and would want more specific information.

Band: 2

Paper 3 Use of English

The FCE Use of English paper contains five parts. There is a total of 65 questions. The time allowed for completion of all five parts, including answer sheet completion, is one hour fifteen minutes.

Test focus

This paper tests the ability of candidates to apply knowledge of the language system. **Parts 1** and **5** focus closely on vocabulary; **Part 4** emphasises grammar and **Parts 2** and **3** focus on both grammar and vocabulary.

Tasks

There are 65 questions in the Use of English paper. Each part of the paper contains a set of questions as follows:

Part 1

A cloze text of approximately 200 words, modified to place emphasis on lexical items, with 15 four-option multiple-choice items.

Part 2

An open cloze text of approximately 200 words, modified to place emphasis on structural words. The text contains 15 gaps to be completed by the candidate. There may be a small number of lexico-grammatical items.

Part 3

A set of ten sentences, each accompanied by a 'key' word and a gapped reformulation of the initial sentence. Candidates are required to complete the gapped sentence, using the key word, so that it has a similar meaning to the prompt sentence.

Part 4

A text of approximately 200 words which contains 15 lines (plus two example lines). Most lines contain errors. The errors are always extra and unnecessary words. Candidates are required to recognise the errors. No line contains more than one error.

Part 5

A text of approximately 150 words which contains ten gaps. Each gap corresponds to a word. The 'stems' of the missing words are given beside the text and must be transformed to provide the missing words.

Marks

One mark is given for each correct answer in **Parts 1, 2, 4** and **5**. For **Part 3,** candidates are awarded a mark of 2, 1 or 0 for each question according to the accuracy of their response. Correct spelling is required in Parts 2, 3 and 5. The total mark is subsequently weighted to 40.

Marking

Part 1 of the Use of English paper is directly scanned by computer. The other parts of the paper are marked under the supervision of a co-ordinating examiner. A mark scheme is drawn up in the light of pre-testing. This is adjusted at the beginning of the marking procedure to take account of actual candidate performance and then finalised. All scripts are double-marked. Question papers may be scrutinised during the marking if there is any doubt about candidate responses on the answer sheets.

Paper 4   Listening

The Listening paper is divided into four parts and is approximately 40 minutes in length. Each part contains a recorded text or texts and corresponding comprehension tasks. There is a total of 30 questions in the Listening paper. Each text is heard twice.

Recordings contain a variety of accents corresponding to standard variants of English native-speaker accent, and to English non-native speaker accents that approximate to the norms of native-speaker accents. Background sounds may be included before speaking begins, to provide contextual information.

The instructions which begin each section of the Listening paper are written and spoken. They give the general context for the input and explain the task.

Candidates are advised to write their answers on the question paper while listening. Five minutes are allowed at the end of the test for them to transfer their answers to an answer sheet.

Texts

Different text types appropriate to the particular test focus are used in each part of the paper. They may be any of the following types:

Monologues:
- answerphone/free phone messages
- commentaries
- documentaries/features
- instructions
- lectures
- news
- public announcements
- publicity/advertisements
- reports
- speeches
- stories/anecdotes
- talks

Interacting speakers:
- chats
- conversations
- discussions
- interviews
- quizzes
- radio plays
- transactions

Part 1 consists of eight short, unrelated extracts of approximately 30 seconds which may be in the form of monologues or conversations. **Part 2** is a monologue or text involving interacting speakers and lasts approximately 3 minutes. **Part 3** consists of five short related extracts of approximately 30 seconds each. They may be in the form of monologues or exchanges between interacting speakers. **Part 4** is also a monologue or text involving interacting speakers and lasts approximately 3 minutes.

Test focus

The tasks in the Listening paper test candidates' ability to:

Parts 1 and 3

Understand gist, main points, function, location, roles and relationships, mood, attitude, intention, feeling or opinion.

Parts 2 and 4

Understand gist, main points, detail or specific information, or deduce meaning.

Tasks

There are 30 questions on the Listening paper. Each listening text is accompanied by a set of questions as follows:

Part	Task	Number of questions
1	Multiple choice	8
2	Note-taking or blank-filling	10
3	Multiple matching	5
4	Selection from 2 or 3 possible answers	7

Task types include note-taking, form-filling, blank-filling or sentence completion for Part 2. In Part 4, questions may have two alternatives or three, e.g. multiple choice, multiple matching and true/false.

Marks

One mark is given for each correct answer. The total is weighted to give a mark out of 40 for the paper. Incorrect spelling is not penalised, provided that the candidates' intention is clear, except where a word has been spelt out letter by letter, for example, a proper name, and where this would actually be a test of the candidates' ability to follow the spelling.

For security reasons, several versions of the Listening paper are used at each administration of the examination. Before grading, the performance of the candidates in each of the versions is compared and marks adjusted to compensate for any imbalance in levels of difficulty.

Marking

Part 1 and **Part 3** of the Listening paper are directly scanned by computer. The other parts of the paper are marked under the supervision of a co-ordinating examiner. A mark scheme for each version of the Listening paper is drawn up in the light of pre-testing. This is adjusted at the beginning of the marking procedure to take account of actual candidate performance, and then finalised. All scripts are double-marked. Question papers may be scrutinised during the marking if there is any doubt about candidates' responses on the answer sheets.

Paper 5   Speaking Test

The FCE Speaking Test is conducted by two examiners (an Interlocutor who will conduct the test and speak to the candidates, and an Assessor who will just listen to the candidates) with pairs of candidates. The test takes fourteen minutes for each pair of candidates and is divided into four parts:

Part 1	Interview	(3 minutes)
Part 2	Individual long turn	(4 minutes)
Part 3	Two-way collaborative task	(3 minutes)
Part 4	Three-way discussion	(4 minutes)

A pair of colour photographs is provided for each candidate as the visual prompts for **Part 2** together with a verbal rubric. The prompts for **Part 3** may be in the form of photographs, line drawings, diagrams, word prompts, etc., together with a verbal rubric. **Parts 1** and **4** do not require visual prompts.

Test focus

Interacting in conversational English in a range of contexts; demonstrating this through appropriate control of grammar and vocabulary, discourse management, pronunciation and interactive communication.

Tasks

The purpose of **Part 1** ('Interview': three minutes) is to test general interactional and social language.

In this part of the test, candidates respond to direct questions asked by the Interlocutor. Candidates are expected to expand on their responses, talking about present circumstances, past experiences and future plans.

The purpose of **Part 2** ('Individual long turn': four minutes) is to elicit a sample of transactional language from each candidate.

In **Part 2** each candidate is given the opportunity to talk without interruption for one minute. Candidates demonstrate their ability to organise their language and ideas with an appropriate use of grammar and vocabulary. Each candidate gives information and expresses opinions through comparing and contrasting two colour photographs.

The purpose of **Part 3** ('Collaborative task': three minutes) is to elicit short transactional turns from each candidate by engaging both of them in the same problem-solving activity.

The tasks are designed to be open and speculative, and to give candidates the opportunity to demonstrate their range of language; the metalanguage of the exchange is as much part of the test as the utterances directly connected with the prompt. All **Part 3** tasks are shared; candidates are encouraged to talk together, without the Interlocutor, and should be able to express and justify their own views, invite the opinions and ideas of their partner and, where necessary or appropriate, negotiate a decision.

The purpose of **Part 4** ('Three-way discussion': four minutes) is to elicit a further sample of speech from the candidates by allowing them to participate in a wider discussion with the Interlocutor of the issues raised or touched on in **Part 3**.

At the end of the Speaking Test, candidates are thanked for attending but are given no indication of their level of achievement.

NB If there is an uneven number of candidates at a session, the last three candidates will be examined together.

Assessment

Throughout the Speaking Test candidates are assessed on their language skills, not their personality, intelligence or knowledge of the world. However, in order to be able to make a fair and accurate assessment of each candidate's performance, the examiners must be given an adequate sample of language to assess. Candidates must, therefore, be prepared to provide full answers to the questions asked by either the Interlocutor or the other candidate, and to speak clearly and audibly. While it is the responsibility of the Interlocutor, where necessary, to manage or direct the interaction, thus ensuring that both candidates are given an equal opportunity to speak, it is the responsibility of the candidates to maintain the interaction as much as possible. Candidates who take equal turns in the interchange will utilise to best effect the amount of time available and provide the examiners with an adequate amount of language to assess.

Marks are awarded throughout the test according to the following assessment criteria (four analytical marks provided by the Assessor, and one global mark provided by the Interlocutor) which together make up the candidate's linguistic profile:

- Grammar and Vocabulary
- Discourse management
- Pronunciation
- Interactive Communication
- Global achievement

Grammar and Vocabulary refers to the accurate and appropriate use of syntactic forms and vocabulary in order to meet the task requirements at an appropriate speed of delivery.

Discourse management refers to the ability to use an appropriate range of linguistic resources to organise sentences to form text. It embraces the concept of coherence, the use of cohesive devices and the appropriate complexity of utterances.

Pronunciation generally refers to the ability to produce comprehensible utterances to fulfil the task requirements. More specifically this refers to the production of individual sounds, appropriate linking of words, word stress, stress timing, highlighting of words to indicate information or to enforce a message, and use of contrasting pitch levels to convey the intended meaning.

NB At FCE level, it is recognised that candidates' pronunciation will be influenced by L1 features.

Interactive Communication refers to the ability to interact in the discourse by responding and initiating appropriately at the required speed and rhythm to fulfil the task requirements.

The Global Achievement Scale refers to the candidate's overall effectiveness in dealing with the four tasks in the test. The Interlocutor is required to give one global mark on this scale for the candidate's performance across all parts of the test.

Candidates are assessed on their own performance according to the established criteria and are not assessed in relation to each other. Assessment is based on performance in the whole test and is not related to performance in particular parts of the test. After initial training of examiners, standardisation of marking is maintained by both biannual examiner co-ordination sessions and by monitoring visits to Centres by Team Leaders. During co-ordination sessions, examiners watch and discuss sample tests recorded on video and then conduct practice Speaking Tests with volunteer candidates in order to establish a common standard of assessment. The sample tests on video are selected to demonstrate a range of task types and different levels of competence, and are pre-marked by a team of experienced examiners.

In many countries, Oral Examiners are assigned to teams, each of which is led by a Team Leader who may be responsible for approximately fifteen Oral Examiners. Team Leaders advise, support and monitor Oral Examiners as required.

The Team Leaders are responsible to a Senior Team Leader within their country, who is the professional representative of UCLES for the oral examinations. Senior Team Leaders are appointed by UCLES and attend an annual co-ordination and development session in the UK. Team Leaders are appointed by the Senior Team Leader in consultation with the local administration.

Grading and results

Grading takes place once all scripts have been returned to UCLES and marking is complete. This is approximately six weeks after the date of the examination. There are two main stages: grading and awards.

Grading

The five FCE papers total 200 marks after weighting. Each paper is weighted to 40 marks.

The overall grade boundaries (A, B, C, D, E and U) are set according to the following information:

- statistics on the candidature
- statistics on the overall candidate performance
- statistics on individual items, for those parts of the examination for which this is appropriate (Papers 1, 3 and 4)
- advice, based on the performance of candidates, and recommendations of examiners, where this is relevant (Papers 2 and 5)
- comparison with statistics from previous years' examination performance and candidature

A candidate's overall FCE grade is based on the total score gained by the candidate in all five papers. It is not necessary to achieve a satisfactory level in all five papers in order to pass the examination.

Awards

The Awarding Committee meets after the grade boundaries have been confirmed. It deals with all cases presented for special consideration, e.g., temporary disability, unsatisfactory examination conditions, suspected collusion, etc. The committee can decide to ask for scripts to be re-marked, to check results, to change grades, to withhold results, etc. Results may be withheld because of infringement of regulations or because further investigation is needed. Centres are notified if a candidate's results have been scrutinised by the Awarding Committee.

Results

Results are reported as three passing grades (A, B and C) and three failing grades (D, E and U – unclassified). The minimum successful performance which a candidate typically requires in order to achieve a grade C corresponds to about 60% of the total marks. Results slips for those candidates who achieve a pass grade provide an indication of those papers in which an outstanding performance has been achieved. Results slips for those candidates who fail with grade D and E provide an indication of those papers in which performance is particularly weak.

Results slips are issued through centres approximately two months after the examination has been taken.

Certificates are issued about six weeks after the issue of results slips.

Enquiries about results may be made through Local Secretaries, within a month of the issue of results slips.

Paper 5 frameworks

Test 1

Note: In the examination, there will be both an Assessor and an Interlocutor in the room.

The following rubrics use plural forms, where appropriate, although it is realised that a teacher may often be working with an individual student for practice sessions.

The visual material for **Test 1** appears on pages C1, C3 and C5 of the Student's Book.

Part 1 (3 minutes)

Introductions

Interlocutor: Good morning (afternoon/evening). Could I have your mark sheets, please? Thank you.
My name is .... and this is my colleague ....
He/she is just going to be listening to us.
So, you are .... and ....? Thank you.
First of all we'd like to know something about you, so I'm going to ask you some questions about yourselves.

(Select one or more questions from each of the following categories as appropriate.)

Home Town

Interlocutor: Let's begin with your home town or village.

- Where are you from?
- Can you tell me something about (*candidate's town or village*)?
- What is there to do in the evenings in (*candidate's town or village*)?
- Which part of your town/village do you like most? Why?
- What kind of jobs do the people in your town/village do?

Family

Interlocutor: And what about your family?

- Do you have a large family or a small family?
- Can you tell me something about them?

Work/Study

Interlocutor: And what about you?

- Can you tell me something about yourself?
- Do you work or are you a student?
- What do you enjoy most about your work/studies?
- What qualifications did you need/will you need for your job/for the job you hope to do?

Leisure

Interlocutor: Now, let's move on to what you do in your spare time.

- Do you have any hobbies?
- How did you become interested in (*whatever hobby the candidate enjoys*)?
- Which do you prefer more, watching television or going to the cinema? What sort of programmes/films do you like to watch?
- What kind of sports are you and your friends interested in?
- What kind of music do you enjoy most?
- How do you usually spend your holidays?
- Is there anywhere you would particularly like to visit? Why?

Future Plans

Interlocutor: Now, thinking about the future.

- What do you hope to do in the next few years?
- How important is English for your future plans?
- What do you hope to be doing in five years' time?

Part 2 (4 minutes)

Interlocutor: Now, I'd like each of you to talk on your own for about a minute.
I'm going to give each of you two different photographs and I'd like you to talk about them. Candidate A, here are your two photographs. They show friends enjoying themselves in different places. Please let Candidate B have a look at them.

Indicate pictures 1A and 1B to Candidate A.

Candidate B, I'll give you your photographs in a minute.

Candidate A, I'd like you to compare and contrast these photographs saying where you like to go with your friends. Remember, you have only about a minute for this so don't worry if I interrupt you. All right?

Candidate A: [*Approximately one minute.*]

Interlocutor: Thank you.
Candidate B, would you tell us which of these places you would prefer to be in, please?

Candidate B: [*Approximately twenty seconds.*]

Interlocutor: Thank you.
Now, Candidate B, here are your photographs. They show people reading different types of publications. Please let Candidate A have a look at them.

Indicate pictures 1C and 1D to Candidate B.

I'd like you to compare and contrast these photographs saying what sort of books or magazines you enjoy reading. Remember, Candidate B, you have only about a minute for this, so don't worry if I interrupt you.

Candidate B: [*Approximately one minute.*]

Interlocutor: Thank you.

Candidate A, would you tell us what kind of books you prefer to read, please?

Candidate A: [*Approximately twenty seconds.*]

Interlocutor: Thank you.

Part 3 (3 minutes)

Interlocutor: Now, I'd like you to do something together. I'm just going to listen.

I'd like you to imagine that your local council has decided to develop a piece of wasteland on the outskirts of this/your town and you have been asked for your opinion. Here are three of the plans that have been put forward.

Indicate picture 1E to the candidates.

Please talk to each other about how each of the suggestions might affect the local population, which group of people might benefit most from the development, and then try to reach an agreement about which suggestion would be best for the area.

All right?

You have only about three minutes for this, so, once again, don't worry if I stop you and please speak so that we can hear you.

Candidates A & B: [*Approximately three minutes.*]

Interlocutor: Thank you.

Part 4 (4 minutes)

Select any of the following questions as appropriate to encourage further discussion.

Interlocutor: Which suggestion would be the least popular for the area in which you live?

Do you have any new developments in your area? If so, how successful are they?

How useful do you think it is to have supermarkets outside the city centre?

How important do you think it is to create wildlife parks?

What sort of leisure facilities are there in your area?

Thank you. That is the end (of the test).

Test 2

Note: In the examination, there will be both an Assessor and an Interlocutor in the room.

The following rubrics use plural forms, where appropriate, although it is realised that a teacher may often be working with an individual student for practice sessions.

The visual material for **Test 2** appears on pages C2, C4 and C6 of the Student's Book.

Part 1 (3 minutes)

Introductions

Interlocutor: Good morning (afternoon/evening). Could I have your mark sheets, please? Thank you.
My name is .... and this is my colleague ....
He/she is just going to be listening to us.
So, you are .... and ....? Thank you.
First of all we'd like to know something about you, so I'm going to ask you some questions about yourselves.

(*Select one or more questions from each of the following categories as appropriate.*)

Home Town

Interlocutor: Let's begin with your home town or village.

- Where are you from?
- Can you tell me something about (*candidate's town or village*)?
- What is there to do in the evenings in (*candidate's town or village*)?
- Which part of your town/village do you like most? Why?
- What kind of jobs do the people in your town/village do?

Family

Interlocutor: And what about your family?

- Do you have a large family or a small family?
- Can you tell me something about them?

Work/Study

Interlocutor: And what about you?

- Can you tell me something about yourself?
- Do you work or are you a student?
- What do you enjoy most about your work/studies?
- What qualifications did you need/ will you need for your job/for the job you hope to do?

Leisure

Interlocutor: Now, let's move on to what you do in your spare time.

- Do you have any hobbies?
- How did you become interested in (*whatever hobby the candidate enjoys*)?
- Which do you prefer more, watching television or going to the cinema? What sort of programmes/films do you like to watch?

- What kind of sports are you and your friends interested in?
- What kind of music do you enjoy most?
- How do you usually spend your holidays?
- Is there anywhere you would particularly like to visit? Why?

Future Plans

Interlocutor: Now, thinking about the future.

- What do you hope to do in the next few years?
- How important is English for your future plans?
- What do you hope to be doing in five years' time?

Part 2 (4 minutes)

Interlocutor: Now, I'd like each of you to talk on your own for about a minute.

I'm going to give each of you two different photographs and I'd like you to talk about them. Candidate A, here are your two photographs. They show different types of holidays. Please let Candidate B have a look at them.

Indicate pictures 2A and 2B to Candidate A.

Candidate B, I'll give you your photographs in a minute.

Candidate A, I'd like you to compare and contrast these photographs saying if you prefer active or relaxing holidays. Remember, you have only about a minute for this so don't worry if I interrupt you. All right?

Candidate A: [*Approximately one minute.*]

Interlocutor: Thank you.

Candidate B, would you tell us which of these holidays you would prefer?

Candidate B: [*Approximately twenty seconds.*]

Interlocutor: Thank you.

Now, Candidate B, here are your photographs. They show children playing with different kinds of toys. Please let Candidate A have a look at them.

Indicate pictures 2C and 2D to Candidate B.

I'd like you to compare and contrast these photographs saying whether or not modern toys are better than traditional toys. Remember, Candidate B, you have only about a minute for this, so don't worry if I interrupt you.

Candidate B: [*Approximately one minute.*]

Interlocutor: Thank you.

Candidate A, would you tell us which of these toys you think is better for children, please?

Candidate A: [*Approximately twenty seconds.*]

Interlocutor: Thank you.

Part 3 (3 minutes)

Interlocutor: Now, I'd like you to do something together. I'm just going to listen.

I'd like you to imagine that a competition has been organised to find the International Personality of the Year and you have been asked to recommend a suitable winner. Here are some ideas of the types of people who might win this award but you may have other ideas of your own.

Indicate picture 2E to the candidates.

Talk together about which type of person is the most suitable to win the award and then try to reach an agreement about who the award should go to.

All right?

You have only about three minutes for this, so, once again, don't worry if I stop you and please speak so that we can hear you.

Candidates A & B: [*Approximately three minutes.*]

Interlocutor: Thank you.

Part 4 (4 minutes)

Select any of the following questions as appropriate to encourage further discussion.

Interlocutor: What is the most important quality for a human being to possess? Why do you think this?

If you had to choose a personality from your local community, who would it be? Why would you choose that person?

Would you like to be famous? Why/why not?

What do you think are the negative aspects of being famous?

Which person from the past do you admire most? Why?

Thank you. That is the end (of the test).

Test 3

Note: In the examination, there will be both an Assessor and an Interlocutor in the room.

The following rubrics use plural forms, where appropriate, although it is realised that a teacher may often be working with an individual student for practice sessions.

The visual material for **Test 3** appears on pages C7, C9 and C11 of the Student's Book.

Part 1 (3 minutes)

Introductions

Interlocutor: Good morning (afternoon/evening). Could I have your mark sheets, please? Thank you.
My name is .... and this is my colleague ....
He/she is just going to be listening to us.
So, you are .... and ....? Thank you.
First of all we'd like to know something about you, so I'm going to ask you some questions about yourselves.

(*Select one or more questions from each of the following categories as appropriate.*)

Home Town

Interlocutor: Let's begin with your home town or village.

- Where are you from?
- Can you tell me something about (*candidate's town or village*)?
- What is there to do in the evenings in (*candidate's town or village*)?
- Which part of your town/village do you like most? Why?
- What kind of jobs do the people in your town/village do?

Family

Interlocutor: And what about your family?

- Do you have a large family or a small family?
- Can you tell me something about them?

Work/Study

Interlocutor: And what about you?

- Can you tell me something about yourself?
- Do you work or are you a student?
- What do you enjoy most about your work/studies?
- What qualifications did you need/will you need for your job/for the job you hope to do?

Leisure

Interlocutor: Now, let's move on to what you do in your spare time.

- Do you have any hobbies?
- How did you become interested in (*whatever hobby the candidate enjoys*)?
- Which do you prefer more, watching television or going to the cinema? What sort of programmes/films do you like to watch?

- What kind of sports are you and your friends interested in?
- What kind of music do you enjoy most?
- How do you usually spend your holidays?
- Is there anywhere you would particularly like to visit? Why?

Future Plans

Interlocutor: Now, thinking about the future.

- What do you hope to do in the next few years?
- How important is English for your future plans?
- What do you hope to be doing in five years' time?

Part 2 (4 minutes)

Interlocutor: Now, I'd like each of you to talk on your own for about a minute.

I'm going to give each of you two different photographs and I'd like you to talk about them. Candidate A, here are your two photographs. They show people doing different kinds of jobs. Please let Candidate B have a look at them.

Indicate pictures 3A and 3B to Candidate A.

Candidate B, I'll give you your photographs in a minute.

Candidate A, I'd like you to compare and contrast these photographs saying whether you (would) prefer to work indoors or out-of-doors. Remember, you have only about a minute for this so don't worry if I interrupt you. All right?

Candidate A: [*Approximately one minute.*]

Interlocutor: Thank you.

Candidate B, would you tell us which of these jobs appeals to you more, please?

Candidate B: [*Approximately twenty seconds.*]

Interlocutor: Thank you.

Now, Candidate B, here are your photographs. They show different places where people live. Please let Candidate A have a look at them.

Indicate pictures 3C and 3D to Candidate B.

I'd like you to compare and contrast these photographs saying whether or not they are similar to the type of building you live in. Remember, Candidate B, you have only about a minute for this, so don't worry if I interrupt you.

Candidate B: [*Approximately one minute.*]

Interlocutor: Thank you.

Candidate A, would you tell us which of these buildings you would prefer to live in?

Candidate A: [*Approximately twenty seconds.*]

Interlocutor: Thank you.

Part 3 (3 minutes)

Interlocutor: Now, I'd like you to do something together. I'm just going to listen.

I'd like you to imagine that your local tourist office is producing five leaflets which will be used to give information about this area to visiting students and you have been asked for your opinion. Here are some ideas of things to include in the leaflets but you may have other ideas of your own.

Indicate picture 3E to the candidates.

Please talk to each other about the subjects that you think would interest students, try to reach an agreement about the five most important ones and then suggest how you could make the leaflets attractive.

All right?

You have only about three minutes for this, so, once again, don't worry if I stop you and please speak so that we can hear you.

Candidates A & B: [*Approximately three minutes.*]

Interlocutor: Thank you.

Part 4 (4 minutes)

Select any of the following questions as appropriate to encourage further discussion.

Interlocutor: What other ways are there of presenting information of this kind?

How important is it to include pictures in leaflets of this kind?

How easy is it to obtain information about your town/area?

If you need information about a town you want to visit, where do you go?

In what ways might a series of leaflets for retired people be different?

Thank you. That is the end (of the test).

Test 4

Note: In the examination, there will be both an Assessor and an Interlocutor in the room.

The following rubrics use plural forms, where appropriate, although it is realised that a teacher may often be working with an individual student for practice sessions.

The visual material for **Test 4** appears on pages C8, C10 and C12 of the Student's Book.

Part 1 (3 minutes)

Introductions

Interlocutor: Good morning (afternoon/evening). Could I have your mark sheets, please? Thank you.
My name is .... and this is my colleague ....
He/she is just going to be listening to us.
So, you are .... and ....? Thank you.
First of all we'd like to know something about you, so I'm going to ask you some questions about yourselves.

(Select one or more questions from each of the following categories as appropriate.)

Home Town

Interlocutor: Let's begin with your home town or village.

- Where are you from?
- Can you tell me something about (*candidate's town or village*)?
- What is there to do in the evenings in (*candidate's town or village*)?
- Which part of your town/village do you like most? Why?
- What kind of jobs do the people in your town/village do?

Family

Interlocutor: And what about your family?

- Do you have a large family or a small family?
- Can you tell me something about them?

Work/Study

Interlocutor: And what about you?

- Can you tell me something about yourself?
- Do you work or are you a student?
- What do you enjoy most about your work/studies?
- What qualifications did you need/will you need for your job/for the job you hope to do?

Leisure

Interlocutor: Now, let's move on to what you do in your spare time.

- Do you have any hobbies?
- How did you become interested in (*whatever hobby the candidate enjoys*)?
- Which do you prefer more, watching television or going to the cinema? What sort of programmes/films do you like to watch?

- What kind of sports are you and your friends interested in?
- What kind of music do you enjoy most?
- How do you usually spend your holidays?
- Is there anywhere you would particularly like to visit? Why?

Future Plans

Interlocutor: Now, thinking about the future.
- What do you hope to do in the next few years?
- How important is English for your future plans?
- What do you hope to be doing in five years' time?

Part 2 (4 minutes)

Interlocutor: Now, I'd like each of you to talk on your own for about a minute.

I'm going to give each of you two different photographs and I'd like you to talk about them. Candidate A, here are your two photographs. They show people enjoying music in different ways. Please let Candidate B have a look at them.

Indicate pictures 4A and 4B to Candidate A.

Candidate B, I'll give you your photographs in a minute.

Candidate A, I'd like you to compare and contrast these photographs saying what sort of music you prefer to listen to. Remember, you have only about a minute for this so don't worry if I interrupt you. All right?

Candidate A: [*Approximately one minute.*]

Interlocutor: Thank you.

Candidate B, would you tell us what kind of music you enjoy, please?

Candidate B: [*Approximately twenty seconds.*]

Interlocutor: Thank you.
Now, Candidate B, here are your photographs. They show people keeping fit in different ways. Please let Candidate A have a look at them.

Indicate pictures 4C and 4D to Candidate B.

I'd like you to compare and contrast these photographs saying what you do to keep healthy. Remember, Candidate B, you have only about a minute for this, so don't worry if I interrupt you.

Candidate B: [*Approximately one minute.*]

Interlocutor: Thank you.

Candidate A, would you tell us if you have ever taken part in activities like these, please?

Candidate A: [*Approximately twenty seconds.*]

Interlocutor: Thank you.

Part 3 (3 minutes)

Interlocutor: Now, I'd like you to do something together. I'm just going to listen.

I'd like you to imagine that a television company is going to produce a one-hour television programme about fashion and you have been asked to help plan the programme. Here are some ideas of things you might like to include but you may have other ideas of your own.

Indicate picture 4E to the candidates.

Talk together and try to reach an agreement about which four areas of fashion to include in the programme. Suggest which group or groups of people it might appeal to and say how you would plan the programme.

All right?

You have only about three minutes for this, so, once again, don't worry if I stop you and please speak so that we can hear you.

Candidates A & B: [*Approximately three minutes.*]

Interlocutor: Thank you.

Part 4 (4 minutes)

Select any of the following questions as appropriate to encourage further discussion.

Interlocutor: What sort of fashion programmes do you watch in your country?

What type of music is popular among young people in your country?

How much do you think young people are influenced by film stars/pop stars/fashion models?

What is the most fashionable thing to own among young people in your country nowadays? Why do you think it is so popular?

How have styles in make-up/hair changed in your country in the last five years?

Thank you. That is the end (of the test).

Test 1 Key

Paper 1 Reading (1 hour 15 minutes)

Part 1
1 F   2 H   3 A   4 C   5 G   6 D   7 B

Part 2
8 C   9 A   10 B   11 D   12 A   13 B   14 C

Part 3
15 G   16 E   17 A   18 B   19 H   20 F   21 D

Part 4
22 B   23 A   24 D   25/26 B/C *(in any order)*   27 D   28 A
29 E   30 B   31 E   32 A   33 B   34 C   35 E

Paper 2 Writing (1 hour 30 minutes)

Task-specific mark schemes

Question 1
Content
Letter should enquire about disco availability for 9 July, giving times (8.30–12) and location (Ambrose Hotel). Mention of the number of people expected to attend (about 40). Questions about the cost and whether David Price can organise competitions for best dancers, etc. Should also specify the type of music wanted. Relevant additional information should be credited.

Organisation and cohesion
Clear paragraphing. Early reference to the disco. Ending suitable to a letter of request.

Register and format
Formal letter (though a more informal register would be acceptable if the letter began 'Dear David').

Range
Future tenses. Polite requests. Vocabulary to do with entertainment and parties.

Target reader
Would have a clear idea of the nature of the work and be able to respond.

Question 2 Report

Content
Report on the shops available locally in candidate's own town. Should include reference to more than one different type of shop and give useful factual information, such as what students can buy, quality of goods, opening times, etc.

Range
Language of description. Language of advice and suggestion. Possibly some personal opinion, though this should be subsidiary to the factual language. Vocabulary relevant to shops and shopping.

Organisation and cohesion
Clear paragraphs and possibly sub-headings.

Register and format
Informal or neutral (student readers); layout appropriate to a report.

Target reader
Would have enough details to know where to shop in the area.

Question 3 Informal letter

Content
Description of the people the writer is with, details of what he/she has done so far and some indication of plans for the coming week.

Range
Past and future tenses. Language of description. Phrases to convey enthusiasm (or lack of enthusiasm).

Organisation and cohesion
Clear flow and suitable paragraphing. Appropriate ending to an informal letter.

Register and format
Informal letter.

Target reader
Would be pleased to hear from the friend and have a detailed picture of what the holiday was like.

Question 4 Composition

Content
Personal opinions on the influence of violent films/TV on young people. Preferably some examples given, to illustrate the opinions.

Range
Phrases to introduce an argument or opinion. Adjectives describing violent/bad behaviour. Habitual present tense. Possibly some use of conditional tenses.

Organisation and cohesion
Clear paragraphing and some form of introduction. Effective use of linking devices. Each new idea in a separate paragraph. Strong conclusion.

Register and format
Neutral, conventional composition layout.

Target reader
Would have a clear picture of the writer's opinions.

Question 5 Background reading texts

(a)
Content
Two places to be named.
Explanation of choice.

Range
Language of description/summarising and explanation.

Organisation and cohesion
Linking of description, summary and explanation.

Appropriacy of register and format
Neutral: composition layout.

Target reader
Would understand why the writer thinks the chosen places are important to the book/story.

(b)
Content
Summary of development of story. Explanation of parts that are easy to follow and parts that are not.

Range
Language of summary, opinion and explanation.

Organisation and cohesion
Linking of summary opinion and explanation.

Appropriacy of register and format
The article should be more or less formal given the intended readership, but consistency is important.

Target reader
Would understand why the writer thinks some parts of the story are easy/difficult to follow.

Paper 3 Use of English (1 hour 15 minutes)

Part 1

1 A   2 D   3 A   4 B   5 B   6 C   7 A   8 D   9 A
10 B   11 B   12 C   13 A   14 C   15 A

Part 2

16 this/that   **17** in   **18** to/for   **19** but   **20** date   **21** be
22 not   **23** make/be   **24** what/everything/all   **25** and
26 well/much   **27** on/with   **28** out   **29** which/the (*allow* what)
30 most/more

Part 3

Award one mark for each correct section.
31 if/whether (1) we wanted/preferred/would prefer/like (1)
32 can't/don't we go (1) somewhere (1)
33 to avoid (1) queuing/having to queue/the/a/queue (1)
34 make a choice (1) between (1)
35 (he was) disappointed (1) he remained (1)
36 so crowded that (1) there was (1)
37 not cost (1) as/so much as (1)
38 did her homework (1) before watching (1)
39 have (1) run out of (1)
40 is/has been three years (1) since (1)

Part 4

41 of   **42** more   **43** ✓   **44** ✓   **45** ✓   **46** herself   **47** it   **48** to
49 are   **50** with   **51** ✓   **52** the   **53** sure   **54** us   **55** ✓

Part 5

56 Chinese   **57** communication(s)   **58** reliable   **59** births
60 unpleasant   **61** death   **62** warning(s)   **63** commonly
64 religious   **65** celebration(s)

Paper 4 Listening (40 minutes approximately)

Part 1

1 A   **2** B   **3** C   **4** C   **5** A   **6** B   **7** A   **8** C

Part 2

9 Liverpool   **10** 1982   **11** (Dr/Doctor) Jane Brown
12 five/5 glass houses/greenhouses
13 PITCHER(S) (*spelt correctly*) (plants/flowers)   **14** cloud forest
15 fish   **16** Wednesday(s) and Thursday(s)/Weds and Thurs (*both needed*)
17 Free/none/no (charge)   **18** (a/the) banana tree

Part 3

19 D   **20** C   **21** B   **22** F   **23** A

Part 4

24 B   **25** C   **26** B   **27** A   **28** A   **29** B   **30** C

Transcript *First Certificate Listening Test. Test One.*
Hello. I'm going to give you the instructions for this test. I'll introduce each part of the test and give you time to look at the questions. At the start of each piece you'll hear this sound.

tone

You'll hear each piece twice.

Remember, while you're listening, write your answers on the question paper. You'll have time at the end of the test to copy your answers onto the separate answer sheet.

The tape will now be stopped. Please ask any questions now, because you must not speak during the test.

[pause]

PART 1 *Now open your question paper and look at Part One.*
You'll hear people talking in eight different situations. For questions 1 to 8, choose the best answer, A, B or C.

Question 1 *One*
You hear the weather forecast on the radio. What is the weather going to be like today?
A getting brighter
B getting windier
C getting wetter

[pause]

tone

Weather forecaster: Good morning. Well, it's generally a cloudy start to the day with a little bit of rain in places, particularly in the north. But I think things will improve slowly as we go through the day. So, although staying cloudy for most of this morning, I think there's every chance of the sun coming through during the afternoon, especially in the south, and lifting the temperature to around 18 degrees, out of the light to moderate north to northeast wind. The north could turn rather cool this evening, but there is unlikely to be any further rain.

[pause]

tone

[The recording is repeated.]

[pause]

Question 2 *Two*
You are listening to a trailer for a radio programme later this evening. What is the programme about?
A music
B fashion
C films

[pause]

tone

Radio presenter: Tonight at ten tune into Pete Zimmerman's 'Night Moves', an irreverent look at the latest news from the West Coast shows … tonight Pete looks at the latest evening wear and celebrates the return of the coat and tie.

[pause]

tone

[The recording is repeated.]

[pause]

Question 3 *Three*
You hear a woman talking at a meeting about the environment. What is she doing when she speaks?
A issuing a warning
B suggesting a solution
C making a protest

[pause]

tone

Woman: The most shocking thing for me has been realising that we cannot any longer trust a carrot. I was always brought up to think a carrot was a healthy piece of food and I would happily just clean a carrot and give it to my kids without peeling it and I genuinely believed that I was doing them good. So when the government then turns round and says, 'Oh, sorry, we have a problem with pesticides and from now on we think it's safer to peel your carrots,' I decided something must be done about this and that's why I've come along to make my feelings known.

[pause]

tone

[The recording is repeated.]

[pause]

Question 4 *Four*
You hear a woman talking about her job. What is her present job?
A She trains people to use computers.
B She interviews people looking for jobs.
C She designs games to be played on computers.

[pause]

tone

Woman: I got into the industry completely by accident. I originally trained as a teacher but, after a few years of that, I got a bit fed up and gave it up. My degree had been in art and design and I actually went in to a job agency and they said, you know, 'What do you do?' and I said, 'Well, I teach and I draw in my free time' and then the next day they phoned me up saying, 'There's a small computer games firm, would you like to go for an interview?' So, I went along with no experience, having not drawn on computer or anything and I was given a manual and they said, you know, 'There you go, train yourself!'

[pause]

tone

[The recording is repeated.]

[pause]

Question 5   *Five*
You hear part of a radio programme in which listeners can take part in a competition. What is the prize?
A a book
B a film
C a map

[pause]

tone

Radio presenter: So, that's this week's competition. Now, the prize is this wonderful colour edition of 'Discovering Birds'. It's got excellent colour photography and drawings showing the natural habitat of each of the birds and very easy-to-understand diagrams and descriptions. It's small enough to carry round in your pocket and so even someone like me will be able to find and identify these birds in the field, and that's saying something, I can tell you.

[pause]

tone

[The recording is repeated.]

[pause]

Question 6   *Six*
Listen to this woman talking to her friend. What does she think of the new restaurant?
A It has good service.
B It has good food.
C It is good value for money.

[pause]

tone

Man: Hi Jane. Have you tried the new restaurant in town yet?
Woman: Yes, I went there last night with my mother.
Man: What did you think of it? I may be going this weekend.

Woman:	Well, it's a good job we weren't in a hurry because it took ages for the food to arrive. But when it finally did I have to say that it certainly was worth waiting for.
Man:	And what about the price?
Woman:	Well, it did cost rather more than we were expecting to pay. I think it'll be a while before we go back there.

[pause]

tone

[The recording is repeated.]

[pause]

Question 7 Seven

Listen to this man talking to his friend. Why is he talking to her?
A to postpone a tennis game
B to arrange a dinner party
C to request some help

[pause]

tone

Man:	Hi Brigitte.
Woman:	Hi Dave. I hope you're not planning to cancel our game.
Man:	Ah. Well some friends of mine have just called and they're coming down to see me tomorrow. I haven't seen them for a while and – well – they've helped me a lot in the past. I'd like to return the favour by cooking dinner for them. It means I'll be busy tomorrow.
Woman:	Oh dear – that's a pity. I was looking forward to playing.
Man:	Well – what about the following day – same time?
Woman:	That's fine by me.
Man:	OK. See you then.

[pause]

tone

[The recording is repeated.]

[pause]

Question 8 Eight

Listen to this woman talking about an interview. How does she feel about it?
A confident
B annoyed
C disappointed

[pause]

tone

| Woman: | Well, I felt it was the right kind of job for me. I mean, I had the right qualifications and experience and I really thought I could do the job well. But – I don't know – they asked |

me all the right questions but I think I was just too nervous. I seemed to be saying all the wrong things. I tried hard to make them want me but I could tell it just wasn't going very well. If only I could have a second chance.

[pause]

tone

[The recording is repeated.]

[pause]

That's the end of Part One.
Now turn to Part Two.

PART 2   *You'll hear a radio talk about a new educational and tourist attraction in the north of England. For questions 9 to 18, complete the notes which summarise what the speaker says.*

You now have forty-five seconds in which to look at Part Two.

[pause]

tone

Woman: Here we are today at the unique Saxon Bridge Rainforest Centre located near Liverpool. This is perhaps the last place you'd expect to find a tropical rainforest! Saxon Bridge was started in 1982 – so it's well-established now – by Dr Jane Brown who wanted to educate the British public about the problem of the world's most complex environment.

She's created a whole forest in five glass houses. She started with just one thousand species but the forest now has ten times that number. The most striking are probably the beautiful passion flowers and a weird and wonderful plant called a – and you can't see them so I'll just spell that for you – a pitcher that's P-I-T-C-H-E-R – so named because they carry water like a small vase.

Each of the five houses has its own specialist vegetation and climate: for example the first reproduces the conditions of lowland forest, while the fifth recreates the environment of the cloud forest. Many of the plants are in danger of extinction. Saxon Bridge's aim is to cultivate them so that they might be saved for future generations.

Although the main base is plant life, the Centre also has a representation of birds, reptiles and small mammals including twenty species of small monkeys. The Centre aims to expand its wildlife to include fish. However, it should be emphasised that this is not a zoo. The real scientific focus is on the preservation of endangered plants. The animals are there because of the role they play in completing the forest system.

If you're interested in visiting Saxon Bridge, you should note its special opening times. Because it's mainly an educational institution, certain days of the week are reserved especially for school parties and scientists: that's Mondays, Wednesdays and Thursdays. Saturdays, Sundays and Tuesdays are for the general public. Admission is free for school parties, children under three and wheelchair users. All others pay three pounds.

Saxon Bridge is very easy to find from the motorway because there are plenty of large green signposts with the Centre's symbol – the banana tree – clearly visible.'

[pause]

tone

Now you'll hear Part Two again.

[The recording is repeated.]

[pause]

That's the end of Part Two.
Now turn to Part Three.

PART 3   *You'll hear five different people talking about a drama group which they are members of. For questions 19 to 23, choose which of the statements A to F best summarises what each speaker is saying. Use the letters only once. There is one extra letter which you do not need to use.*

You now have thirty seconds in which to look at Part Three.

[pause]

tone

Speaker 1:   Well, I retired three years ago now and, at first I missed work terribly after twenty-six years, you know, I had nothing to do with myself, it affected me psychologically really. Anyway, I looked round and thought, 'I've got to start something fresh, do something differently'. And so I was looking through this booklet and I saw there was a drama group starting up locally and so I thought, 'I'll give it a try', I've always been a bit of a show off, you know.

[pause]

Speaker 2:   The way I see it, it's like a journey. There are five friends who do everything together. At the beginning one of us is missing, she's had an accident and we go to find her in hospital and see what's the matter with her, and anyway she disappears from there and we all get a bit worried and so set out on this journey to find her, and it sort of develops from there. It's not really like anything we've put on before actually, so there were one or two who needed convincing to go ahead with it.

[pause]

Speaker 3:   Very exciting. I mean when I first joined, I mean, I hadn't done anything at school, I'd never been to other groups or anything whatsoever. I came in because a friend said 'Oh, go on, come' and I thought, 'Well I'll go just once and see,' you know. I ended up being talked into taking the lead in the play that they were doing, never mind just joining the group. I was absolutely terrified, but I enjoyed it so much that I've continued ever since because, well, I mean, it is great fun.

[pause]

Speaker 4:   Well, it's not my first time on stage, that must have been when I was about thirteen, I was to sing in front of all my friends and, I'd had a few lessons, like, but I walked on to that stage and opened my mouth and nothing came out, I just dried up. I can laugh about it now, but it put me off for a good few years, I can tell you. These days, working with the group, I've learnt not to take any notice of the audience or anything like that because when you get to the age I am now people don't expect anything of you, so what you actually do is a pleasant surprise for them.

[pause]

Speaker 5: I've been with this group four years. Umm, I've always done a lot of drama, you know, in different groups, just the usual sort of amateur thing, you know, but I happened to see an advert for this one and came along to give it a try. It was a new play they were doing and it was probably one of the greatest challenges I've faced so far because it was like nothing I'd ever done before and, you know, the people are very imaginative and open to new ideas and in that sense I couldn't wish for anything better.

[pause]

tone

Now you'll hear Part Three again.

[The recording is repeated.]

[pause]

That's the end of Part Three.
Now turn to Part Four.

PART 4   *You will hear an interview with a man who has just returned from travelling. For questions 24 to 30, choose the best answer A, B or C.*

You now have one minute in which to look at Part Four.

[pause]

tone

Interviewer: Welcome to the programme. I have with me in the studio today, Steve Sedley, who's just returned from a rather unusual trip. Steve, how does it feel now you're back?

Steve: Absolutely marvellous ... well, of course I had a wonderful time and I wouldn't have missed it for anything ... but!

Interviewer: I'm sure everyone asks you this question but ... what drives anyone to take time out from a successful career in banking to make such a journey?

Steve: Well ... as a child I read a great many books about the explorers to the South Pole and the great travellers who crossed Europe and Asia ... I wanted to follow in their footsteps in my own small way ... Africa has always fascinated me so I decided to walk from south to north. The money I collected for charity made it worthwhile for other people but to be honest it was the fact that I had become disabled after a childhood illness and well ... I just wanted to show the world what I, as a disabled person, could do.

Interviewer: Yes ... indeed ... well you certainly did that. How long was your journey in total?

Steve: Well ... all in all it took two years and one month. It would have taken less time but I decided to stopover in one place for a few months.

Interviewer: Was that because you were sick?

Steve: I was only ill once on the whole trip and that was for one day ... no, it was because I made friends with a guy I met on the road and he asked me to stay and work with his family to help bring in the harvest and the rest of the stuff around the farm ... I really enjoyed the physical labour and the company of course ... I was very reluctant to leave!

Interviewer: Yes ... And how did your family feel about the trip?

Steve: Well, now they're quite proud and happy about it but I'm sure they'd be the first to admit that before I went they weren't sure what my motives were ... here was this well-paid executive ... loving his creature comforts ... going into the bush.

Interviewer: What was the worst thing that happened to you?

Steve: Undoubtedly when I was suspected of smuggling – there was this officer at the border of ... mentioning no names, who said unless I paid a fine he would hand me over to the police.

Interviewer: How did you get out of it?

Steve: Well ... luckily there was a journalist from a respected local newspaper who saw the incident and threatened to expose the guy ...

Interviewer: That was lucky ...

Steve: It certainly was ... it renewed my respect for the profession 'cos I used to have a very low opinion of the media ... Actually, I can't get over how well my journey has been covered in the press ... after all ... lots of people do it ... I can't see what's so special about my efforts.

Interviewer: One final question ... would you do it all again?

Steve: Well, not exactly the same experience but I wouldn't mind trying it on a motorbike ... now I'm getting older, it might be easier to handle!

Interviewer: Well, the best of luck to you with that. Thank you very much ... Steve Sedley ...

[pause]

tone

Now you'll hear Part Four again.

[The recording is repeated.]

[pause]

That is the end of Part Four.

There'll now be a pause of five minutes for you to copy your answers onto the separate answer sheet. I'll remind you when there is one minute left, so that you're sure to finish in time.

[pause]

You have one more minute left.

[pause]

That's the end of the test. Please stop now. Your supervisor will now collect all the question papers and answer sheets.
Goodbye.

Test 2 Key

Paper 1 Reading (1 hour 15 minutes)

Part 1
1 E   2 C   3 G   4 D   5 A   6 F   7 H

Part 2
8 C   9 A   10 B   11 D   12 A   13 D   14 C

Part 3
15 F   16 A   17 H   18 G   19 D   20 C   21 B

Part 4
22 C   23 D   24 B   25 A   26/27 C/D *(in any order)*   28 D
29/30 A/E *(in any order)*   31 A   32 E   33 B   34 C   35 B

Paper 2 Writing (1 hour 30 minutes)

Task-specific mark schemes

Question 1
Content
The letter should give the friend clear details about the start of term, including registration, bookshop (and own offer), first lesson, party, adding relevant advice, credit given for additional relevant information/suggestions.

Organisation and cohesion
Suitable paragraphing, giving information in a clear sequence.

Register and format
Informal letter.

Range
Language of advice and suggestion. Vocabulary relating to learning English abroad.

Target reader
Would be pleased to hear from the friend, be fully informed and reassured about going on the course.

Question 2 Article

Content

Article should give writer's own opinions and advice about how to study successfully, covering the points in the rubric: study plans; good places to work in; exam preparation; making best use of leisure time.

Range

Language of opinion. Language of advice and suggestion. Possibly some conditional structures. Vocabulary relating to study and education.

Organisation and cohesion

Clear presentation of ideas. Summary conclusion, to underline own opinion.

Register and format

Semi-formal or informal, directed at new students. Article should attempt to engage the reader.

Target reader

Would gain good advice and be interested in the article.

Question 3 Application

Content

Application for waiter/waitress job should say why the candidate is right for the position, giving relevant background, about character, language(s) fitness.

Range

Personal description. Modal verbs. Vocabulary relating to work and catering.

Organisation and cohesion

Appropriate opening and closing formulae, with early reference to the advertisement. Logical presentation of information.

Register and format

Formal letter of application.

Target reader

Would consider the application seriously.

Question 4 Story

Content

Narrative, beginning or ending with the sentence given.

Range

Past tenses.

Organisation and cohesion

Link with the given sentence. Logical sequencing of the action. Story may only have minimal paragraphing.

Register and format

Neutral.

Target reader

Would find the story interesting.

Question 5 Background reading texts

(a)
Content
Brief summary of story. Statement of whether story will be popular or not, and explanation/justification of view.

Range
Language of summarising and explanation.

Organisation and cohesion
Linking of summary and explanation.

Appropriacy of register and format
Neutral; composition layout.

Target reader
Would understand why the writer thinks the story will or will not be popular in 100 years' time.

(b)
Content
Statement of which person in the book is most interesting to the writer. Description of the chosen person's character and an explanation of why the writer finds this person especially interesting.

Range
Language of description and explanation.

Organisation and cohesion
Linking of description and explanation.

Appropriacy of register and format
The article could be more or less formal given the intended readership, but consistency is important.
Article format, with clear opening and appropriate ending.

Target reader
Would understand why the writer thinks the person chosen is the most interesting character in the book.

Paper 3 Use of English (1 hour 15 minutes)

Part 1

1 A	2 D	3 B	4 D	5 C	6 D	7 C	8 B
9 A	10 B	11 A	12 D	13 B	14 A	15 C	

Part 2

16 were   17 the/some   18 to   19 doing   20 his
21 great/good   22 in   23 had   24 be   25 for
26 that/which/and   27 by   28 an   29 few   30 of

Part 3

Award one mark for each correct section.
31 the end (1) of the course (1)
32 if you (1) aren't/are/'re not (1)
33 might/could/may be difficult (1) to find (1)
34 meals are included (1) in the (1)
35 there are (1) two reasons why (1)
36 accused Richard of (1) breaking/having broken (1)
37 can't/cannot (1) keep up/pace with (1)
38 me how (1) to get/I can get (1)
39 not as/so (1) well paid as (1)
40 don't/do not mind (1) which film (1)

Part 4

41 it   42 too   43 do   44 the   45 have   46 ✓   47 ✓
48 variety   49 ✓   50 so   51 to   52 up   53 ✓
54 type   55 who

Part 5

56 following   57 drivers   58 directions   59 previously
60 failure   61 manager   62 unsatisfactory   63 apologised
64 ambitious   65 confident

Paper 4 Listening (40 minutes approximately)

Part 1

1 A   2 B   3 A   4 C   5 B   6 C   7 A   8 B

Part 2

9 Paula (**not** Paul) JAKES (*spelt correctly*)   10 History and Politics (*both needed*)
11 non-user   12 (basic) word(-)processing (skills)   13 speaking dictionary/ies
14 recorded newspapers   15 (£)300 – (£)500   16 Dr Stone   17 225431
18 radio (advert)

Part 3

19 F   20 D   21 B   22 E   23 A

Part 4

24 T   25 F   26 T   27 T   28 F   29 F   30 T

Transcript *First Certificate Listening Test. Test Two.*
Hello. I'm going to give you the instructions for this test. I'll introduce each part of the test and give you time to look at the questions. At the start of each piece you'll hear this sound.

tone

You'll hear each piece twice.

Remember, while you're listening, write your answers on the question paper. You'll have time at the end of the test to copy your answers onto the separate answer sheet.

The tape will now be stopped. Please ask any questions now, because you must not speak during the test.

[pause]

PART 1   *Now open your question paper and look at Part One.*
You'll hear people talking in eight different situations. For questions 1 to 8, choose the best answer, A, B or C.

Question 1   One
You overhear two friends talking about going to a party. When is it?
A   tonight
B   tomorrow night
C   next week

[pause]

tone

Woman:	You must come … Alan'll be really disappointed if you don't.
Man:	But I've got my exams all next week.
Woman:	But it only means missing one night's revision …
Man:	Well … how are we going to get there?
Woman:	My brother said I can borrow his car … as long as I get it back to him first thing tomorrow.
Man:	Oh, all right then.
Woman:	Great … I'll pick you up in half an hour then.

[pause]

tone

[The recording is repeated.]

[pause]

Question 2   Two
You overhear a customer talking to a saleswoman. What does he want to buy?
A   a shirt
B   a suit
C   a pair of trousers

[pause]

tone

Saleswoman:	They're very nice, aren't they?
Man:	Oh, hello … yes … but I'm looking for something in navy blue.

Saleswoman:	Yes, sir. What size did you want?
Man:	I'm forty-two chest and thirty-two waist.
Saleswoman:	Right … well, actually we have a nice one in the window … if you'd like to try it.
Man:	Can I just try on the jacket … and then if I like it, I'll try the trousers as well.
Saleswoman:	Certainly sir.

[pause]

tone

[The recording is repeated.]

[pause]

Question 3   *Three*
Listen to this woman talking to her friend. What is her intention?
A   to request
B   to persuade
C   to suggest

[pause]

tone

Jane:	Phil.
Phil:	Yes?
Jane:	Pass me the sugar, will you? I can't bear coffee without it.
Phil:	Sure. Here you are.
Jane:	Thanks.

[pause]

tone

[The recording is repeated.]

[pause]

Question 4   *Four*
Listen to this extract from a radio programme. What sort of programme is it?
A   a weather forecast
B   a travel show
C   a sports programme

[pause]

tone

| Cricket commentator: | Unfortunately, it's raining at the moment but we've been told that it'll definitely be fine and sunny tomorrow and we expect an exciting game. We're almost at the end of the tour – it's been a hectic few weeks, we've visited no less than five countries and played against some of the best teams in the world. |

[pause]

tone

[The recording is repeated.]

[pause]

Question 5 *Five*
You hear a man telling a story about a colleague who had an accident. Where did the accident happen?
A a sporting event
B a music concert
C a play at a theatre

[pause]

tone

Man: Well, I'd never seen anything like it. He must have used so much breath hitting that top note that he blacked out. The first we knew of it, there was a crash and he fell off the stage into the audience. One or two people ran over, but apart from a few bruises he was OK, and he got up and went back to his place, though he couldn't find his trumpet. And anyway, the incredible thing was that, through all this, no one stopped playing and the conductor didn't bat an eyelid!

[pause]

tone

[The recording is repeated.]

[pause]

Question 6 *Six*
You hear a radio advertisement. What is being advertised?
A a disco
B a social club
C a means of transport

[pause]

tone

Announcer: It's the best ride you'll ever have! Jump aboard the party bus, the last word in party events. This is London's first nightclub tour, you get free entry into four discos in the same evening, and the fun continues on the bus as you travel from one to another. Ideal for birthdays, office parties or a night out with friends. For info and bookings call 881543. Group discounts available on request.

[pause]

tone

[The recording is repeated.]

[pause]

Question 7   *Seven*
You hear part of a programme about things to do in New York. What type of
place is being described?
A a museum
B a shop
C a factory

[pause]

tone

Radio presenter: New York has always been a centre of the fashion industry, its importance based around the development of practical styles for modern working life. The exhibition draws from the vast collection of clothes stored here, to provide a record of how New Yorkers have dressed themselves through the ages. The emphasis here, however, is towards the fantastic creations made for the city's social scene, as might be expected.

[pause]

tone

[The recording is repeated.]

[pause]

Question 8   *Eight*
Listen to this man talking to a taxi driver. Where is he going?
A the airport
B the theatre
C the sports club

[pause]

tone

Man: Could you hurry please. I'm a little late. If I don't get there by twelve-thirty, they'll worry that I'm not going to turn up. They'll probably start without me and that'll cause all kinds of problems. It's the first play we've done for a long time, and everyone's nervous. We have to have a good run through the show to give us all some confidence.

[pause]

tone

[The recording is repeated.]

[pause]

That's the end of Part One.
Now turn to Part Two.

PART 2   *You'll hear a telephone conversation where a woman asks for information about different study aids for the blind. For questions 9 to 18, complete the Enquiries Record.*

You now have forty-five seconds in which to look at Part Two.

[pause]

tone

Man:	Good morning, Banshire Blind Society, how can I help you?
Woman:	Oh good morning. I'm ringing to make enquiries about equipment that might be useful for my studies. I've been blind for three years.
Man:	Right.
Woman:	… and I'm just starting a degree course and I wondered if you have any recommendations for equipment that might be useful.
Man:	Yes, certainly madam … what we normally like to do is to take down some details and then we investigate what might be suitable and get back to you.
Woman:	Yes, fine.
Man:	Right. What's your name please?
Woman:	It's Paula Jakes. I'll just spell that for you … J-A-K-E-S.
Man:	Right and what's the course you'll be following?
Woman:	History and Politics.
Man:	History and Politics. OK. And can I just ask about your ability to use Braille? Would you say you were a very good user, a partial user or a non-user?
Woman:	I haven't used it at all, I'm afraid.
Man:	OK, that's no problem. I'll put down 'non-user'. That'll do. What about computers? Have you got any skills in that area?
Woman:	I do have basic word-processing skills.
Man:	Right, well that's certainly helpful. OK then, now did you have any particular types of equipment in mind?
Woman:	Well … I don't know much about it but I was wondering about speaking dictionaries.
Man:	Right … actually we have a lot of new stuff in that area.
Woman:	And possibly recorded newspapers?
Man:	OK. I'll put that down too. And what sort of price range were you thinking of?
Woman:	Well, I thought around three hundred pounds to start with, but if I have to I'm pretty sure I could get a further two hundred pounds if necessary … so up to five hundred pounds really.
Man:	Oh that's fine. There are one or two good products on the market in your range. Now … what I'll do is look through our files and talk to a couple of people and give you a call … What's your number?
Woman:	Well I don't think you can contact me very easily during the day 'cos I'll be at college … I tell you what, could you call my tutor?
Man:	Yes … sure … no problem, but I'd better have his name.
Woman:	HER name actually. It's Dr Stone.
Man:	Stone. That's fine … and the number?
Woman:	OK, it's 225431
Man:	Fine, I've got that … right … I'll be getting the information to you in the next couple of days.
Woman:	Thanks ever so much.
Man:	Before you go, can I just check how you found out about our enquiry service?
Woman:	Oh, yes. It was through the radio advert.
Man:	OK, many thanks. Bye.
Woman:	Bye.

[pause]

tone

Now you'll hear Part Two again.

[The recording is repeated.]

[pause]

That's the end of Part Two.
Now turn to Part Three.

PART 3 *You'll hear an advert for a travel insurance company where five people talk about bad experiences they've had whilst travelling. For questions 19 to 23, choose from the list A to F what each speaker is describing. Use the letters only once. There's one extra letter which you do not need to use.*

You now have thirty seconds in which to look at Part Three.

[pause]

tone

Speaker 1:   It was an old car but it had never broken down … well except for the odd puncture or problem with the brakes … but never when it mattered … so anyway we were really upset when they took it and we had a lot of problems reporting it.

[pause]

Speaker 2:   My wife and I were on a driving holiday in Europe and we were walking along when suddenly we were surrounded by people. When they'd gone, I checked my pocket and somehow they'd managed to take it. It was such a pain spending days trying to get the right papers from the Embassy, and of course we couldn't move on until it was sorted out.

[pause]

Speaker 3:   We were driving up this really steep road and suddenly the engine just stopped for no reason and we were stuck. Luckily, of all things, a police car came past and they organised a pick-up truck and we managed to get down but it was really expensive.

[pause]

Speaker 4:   It was really hot and so … stupidly we just left a crack in the window … but that was enough and the whole lot was gone when we got back. Luckily we had all our important documents and wallets with us in the restaurant and we just had to buy some new things to wear and stuff but that was still pretty expensive.

[pause]

Speaker 5:   It was one of those things that really upset you 'cos you don't know exactly when and where it happened. At some stage I realised it had gone. Anyway, I didn't have any insurance so I just had to forget about it but I had to spend ages trying to contact my bank to send me out some more.

[pause]

tone

Now you'll hear Part Three again.

[The recording is repeated.]

[pause]

That is the end of Part Three.
Now turn to Part Four.

PART 4   *You'll hear part of a radio programme about a problem caused by birds in a seaside town. For questions 24 to 30, decide whether the statements are TRUE or FALSE. Write T for True or F for False.*

You now have one minute in which to look at Part Four.

[pause]

tone

Interviewer: A seaside town is at war with a part of its population. The attackers are sea birds who have got a taste for fast food. Anything, in fact, they can get from the tourists enjoying an open-air lunch on the seafront. I spoke to some people who'd been attacked.

Tourist: My husband had just got me a burger, and I'd had one bite out of it, and a bird came right up close and whipped it away from me, from my hand. And then there was a little boy, they'd just got him some fish and chips and that, and the bird came and whipped it all away, the whole tray, and the poor little kid, I felt so sorry for him, because it was a horrible experience, even for me, you know.

Interviewer: All around the harbour here, you'll hear the same stories. The Town Council have been trying to do something about the problem, Malcolm Vale is the Town Clerk and he's with me now. So is Jenny Samson, an expert on sea birds. Malcolm, hasn't this always been a problem?

Malcolm: Unfortunately, it's a problem that's developed over a long time. Once upon a time the birds were encouraged by fishermen to come in and clean their nets. The town has always been a source of food for them; they steal from rubbish bins, some people used to feed them.

Interviewer: What action have you taken?

Malcolm: We've had signs put up asking the public not to feed them. The more people that feed them, the more birds we're going to have and the more this will become a way of life for them. We've got the rubbish bins securely covered to deny that as a food source.

Interviewer: Is that going to make any difference, Jenny?

Jenny: Well, the intention's good, but unfortunately if you take away the birds' source of food that may make them more aggressive and certainly it appears that they are getting more desperate to get hold of food, and that's what we are seeing now.

Interviewer: So, Malcolm, is there another solution?

Malcolm: Well, we borrowed an electronic system from an airport which is meant to keep birds away. Just to see if it would work, because they're expensive to buy. And when we first started using it, it was extremely effective, but to a certain extent I think their need for food is probably greater than their sense of danger, because they soon got used to it, and seemed not to take much notice.

Interviewer: Jenny, do you have a solution?

Jenny: Yes, egg pricking can reduce the number of birds.

Interviewer: How does that work?

Jenny: Well, if you prick the eggs, the young will not develop, the young will not be born. It's better to do that than taking the eggs away because that only makes the parent birds lay more eggs.

Interviewer: Malcolm, have you tried this egg pricking?

Malcolm: Oh yes, but remember these birds can live for up to 32 years, so that's a long-term measure. We need something that's going to help us now. It's a very difficult question. We are watching the situation again this summer and we'll be discussing it again, but we may have to find a more direct method of reducing numbers.

[pause]

tone

Now you'll hear Part Four again.

[The recording is repeated.]

[pause]

That is the end of Part Four.

There'll now be a pause of five minutes for you to copy your answers onto the separate answer sheet. I'll remind you when there's one minute left, so that you're sure to finish in time.

[pause]

You have one more minute left.

[pause]

That's the end of the test. Please stop now. Your supervisor will now collect all the question papers and answer sheets.
Goodbye.

Test 3 Key

Paper 1 Reading (1 hour 15 minutes)

Part 1

1 C   2 F   3 D   4 B   5 A   6 E

Part 2

7 C   8 A   9 A   10 B   11 D   12 A   13 C   14 A

Part 3

15 D   16 G   17 B   18 A   19 F   20 E

Part 4

21 E   22 D   23 A   24 A   25 C   26 E   27 C
28 B   29 A   30 C   31 A   32 D   33 B   34 C   35 E

Paper 2 Writing (1 hour 30 minutes)

Task-specific mark schemes

Question 1

Content
Request for information about the boating holidays, asking about the standard of the boats/meaning of 'luxury'; the cost (4 people for 1 week); the distance travelled per day; the cooking equipment provided; any special clothes needed. Relevant additional information should be credited.

Organisation and cohesion
Early reference to the advertisement. Concise description of requirements. Suitable ending.

Register and format
Formal letter.

Range
Phrases to request information. Variety of question forms. Vocabulary relating to boats and holidays.

Target reader
Would have a clear picture of writer's requirements and be able to respond.

Question 2   Story

Content
Narrative, beginning or ending with the sentence given.

Range
Past tenses. Some phrases to describe emotions.

Organisation and cohesion
Link with the given sentence. Story may only have minimal paragraphing.

Register and format
Neutral.

Target reader
Would be interested in the story.

Question 3   Article

Content
Information on the sporting event, which could be something like a tennis tournament or a sports day with different kinds of matches. Should give details of the college's results and what the event was like. Could include facts such as final scores, names of key players, etc. Some reference to the unexpected success.

Range
Past tenses. Factual and descriptive language. Sporting vocabulary.

Organisation and cohesion
Title desirable. Clear paragraphing.

Register and format
Neutral/Informal (article written for the college newspaper).

Target reader
Would be interested and informed.

Question 4   Report

Content
Report should give details of the recent group tour escorting elderly visitors around important buildings, commenting on aspects such as transport, facilities, timing, etc., as well as giving recommendations for similar future tours.

Range
Language of description. Language of suggestion/recommendation. Possibly some personal opinion, though this should be subsidiary to the factual language.

Organisation and cohesion
Clear paragraphs; sub-headings a possibility but not essential.

Register and format
Formal, layout appropriate to a report.

Target reader
Would be informed about the tour and be able to plan future tours.

Question 5 Background reading texts

(a)
Content
Favourite character and actor/actress to be named.
Explanation of choice.

Range
Language of description/summarising and explanation.

Organisation and cohesion
Linking of description/summary and explanation.

Appropriacy of register and format
Neutral; composition layout.

Target reader
Would understand why the writer thinks the chosen actor/actress could play the character chosen.

(b)
Content
Statement and brief summary of events/situations the writer believes could or could not happen in their country nowadays. Explanation of why/why not.

Range
Language of summarising, opinion, and explanation.

Organisation and cohesion
Linking of summary, opinion, and explanation.

Appropriacy of register and format
Neutral; composition layout.

Target reader
Would understand why the writer thinks these events/situations could or could not occur in their country nowadays.

Paper 3 Use of English (1 hour 15 minutes)

Part 1

1 B   2 A   3 C   4 B   5 C   6 A   7 D   8 A   9 C
10 C   11 A   12 A   13 D   14 B   15 A

Part 2

16 from   17 which/that   18 had/needed   19 the   20 out
21 took   22 made   23 that   24 off/out   25 have
26 and   27 what   28 were   29 There   30 been

Part 3

Award one mark for each correct section.
31 went/got/travelled to Liverpool (1) by train (1)
32 without (1) thanking us for our (1)
33 for/(that) there/it will be/to have (1) better (1)
34 's/is responsible (1) for locking (1)
35 had been/was successful (1) in/at giving (1)
36 fell/was asleep (1) as soon/just (1)
37 probably won't/will not (1) see each (1)
38 looking forward to (1) seeing you (1)
39 (can) still remember/recall (1) every/each (1)
40 caused us to (1) get (1)

Part 4

41 that	42 ✓	43 kind	44 ✓	45 done	46 it
47 one	48 them	49 ✓	50 so	51 ✓	52 much
53 the	54 ✓	55 in			

Part 5

56 originally	57 fighters	58 violence	59 respectful
60 inexpensive	61 youngsters	62 instructors	63 demanding
64 strength	65 enjoyable		

Paper 4 Listening (40 minutes approximately)

Part 1

1 B   2 A   3 B   4 B   5 A   6 A   7 C   8 C

Part 2

9 used/second(-)hand   10 (their) money back
11 (they) don't like them/are not/aren't satisfied/unsatisfied
12 electrical (goods)   13 washing machine   14 (someone else's/a) sock
15 display model   16 documents/guarantee/instructions
17 box(es) (not new or)   18 ask (lots of/a lot of) questions

Part 3

19 C   20 F   21 E   22 A   23 D

Part 4

24 T   25 F   26 F   27 T   28 F   29 T   30 F

Transcript *First Certificate Listening Test. Test Three.*
Hello. I'm going to give you the instructions for this test. I'll introduce each part of the test and give you time to look at the questions. At the start of each piece you'll hear this sound.

tone

You'll hear each piece twice.

Remember, while you're listening, write your answers on the question paper. You'll have time at the end of the test to copy your answers onto the separate answer sheet.

The tape will now be stopped. Please ask any questions now, because you must not speak during the test.

[pause]

PART 1   *Now open your question paper and look at Part One.*
You'll hear people talking in eight different situations. For questions 1 to 8, choose the best answer, A, B or C.

Question 1   *One*
Listen to this girl talking about her new boss. How did she feel after she met him?
A   delighted
B   disappointed
C   relieved

[pause]

tone

Girl: So there I was in my best clothes, arrived extra early to make a good impression and guess what? When he turned up I recognised him – yes, we were at school together. The only thing is I couldn't stand him then, he was awful and I bet he hasn't changed. It's going to be really dreadful working under him. I was so looking forward to having a new boss as well.

[pause]

tone

[The recording is repeated.]

[pause]

Question 2   *Two*
You overhear two friends talking about a birthday present one of them has just received. What is it?
A   a television
B   a cassette player
C   a computer

[pause]

tone

Boy 1:   It was a real shock 'cos I hadn't expected anything nearly so expensive!
Boy 2:   Lucky you! Where are you going to put it?
Boy 1:   Well, I thought in the study.

Boy 2:	Why not in your room?
Boy 1:	Well, the reception's quite bad on that side, you get a much better picture at the front.
Boy 2:	Won't it be noisy for your Mum and Dad?
Boy 1:	Oh … they won't mind!

[pause]

tone

[The recording is repeated.]

[pause]

Question 3 *Three*
You overhear two friends talking about a garden party they attended. What was the problem?
A the people
B the weather
C the place

[pause]

tone

Woman 1:	It was pretty awful, wasn't it?
Woman 2:	I know, and it's such a pity because we were all really looking forward to it.
Woman 1:	When everyone had to come rushing in absolutely soaking wet I couldn't believe it!
Woman 2:	It came down so quickly and it had been such a lovely bright morning.
Woman 1:	And that amazing place, the garden and the lovely bright marquee.
Woman 2:	Her family were furious. All that money.

[pause]

tone

[The recording is repeated.]

[pause]

Question 4 *Four*
On a visit to a college, you overhear part of a lesson. What is the subject of the lesson?
A health and safety
B child development
C food preparation

[pause]

tone

Woman:	When you're very young, eating is a hands-on experience. Food is not just a matter of taste and smell, it's feel too. Babies learn by feeling things. It's a way of double-checking on what their eyes can see. So, next time your baby sister splatters you with her dinner, remember it's all part of the learning experience.

[pause]

tone

[The recording is repeated.]

[pause]

Question 5   *Five*
Listen to this critic talking about a film. What sort of film is it?
A   a comedy
B   a romance
C   a thriller

[pause]

tone

Critic: Well, I have to say I thoroughly enjoyed this film. I'm sure it'll be a box office hit this summer. Watch out for Roland Bernz, better known for his roles in action packed adventures, chasing the girls, he's really convincing in his first attempt as a funny man – lots of good lines had the audience laughing to the end.

[pause]

tone

[The recording is repeated.]

[pause]

Question 6   *Six*
Listen to this boy talking to a friend about flying. How does he feel about flying?
A   excited
B   depressed
C   scared

[pause]

tone

Girl: Hi Paul – looking forward to your holiday?
Boy: Oh, yeah – it's going to be great. Though I'm a bit worried that I've packed the wrong clothes. I don't think the weather's going to be as good as I hoped.
Girl: You're flying on Saturday, aren't you?
Boy: That's right – my first flight.
Girl: I was terrified the first time I went in an aeroplane.
Boy: Oh, I can't wait. I bet it'll be the highlight of the trip. I'm only sad that you're not coming with me.
Girl: Maybe next time, Paul.

[pause]

tone

[The recording is repeated.]

[pause]

Question 7   *Seven*
You hear an artist talking about her work. What type of artist is she?
A a photographer
B a sculptor
C a painter

[pause]

tone

Artist: You have to make a person look as if they're alive. You can look at a piece of sculpture and it's very lifelike and has a presence in itself, it already has depth; a picture you have to create from a flat surface. In photography, you know you're always going to get an image anyway. But when I start, I don't even know whether I'm going to manage it. You start off with a white canvas and a tray of paints in front of you and that's all.

[pause]

tone

[The recording is repeated.]

[pause]

Question 8   *Eight*
Listen to this woman leaving a phone message. Why is she phoning?
A She is complaining about something.
B She is requesting something.
C She is apologising about something.

[pause]

tone

Man: This is Dave Edmonds' answerphone. I'm not at home at the moment. Please leave a message after the tone. (beeeeeep)
Woman: Dave, this is Janet. I just remembered that you'd asked me to book a table at the Italian restaurant this evening. I've left it a bit late I'm afraid. I hope you're not going to be too angry. I've just phoned them and they're booked up. I know it's your favourite place. I'm not sure what to do now … I'll speak to you later.

[pause]

tone

[The recording is repeated.]

[pause]

That's the end of Part One.
Now turn to Part Two.

PART 2   *You will hear Ian Anderson of the Shoppers' Association talking about a problem people may face when buying some kinds of goods. For questions 9 to 18, complete the notes.*

You now have forty-five seconds in which to look at Part Two.

[pause]

tone

Ian Anderson: While most people trust that what they buy off the shelf in their local shop will be as described and brand new, there seems to be a growing trade in second-hand goods actually being sold as new. Shoppers' Association members are worried that the increasing number of used goods being discovered on offer in shops represent just the tip of the iceberg. I've dealt with over 40 cases of this kind in my area this year and, as it seems that this practice is on the increase, today's talk is aimed at keeping you all on the look out.

So, why is it happening? I think one of the main reasons is that if customers aren't satisfied with their goods, shops just give them their money back. Now, sometimes the goods are faulty, but clearly customers take advantage of this for all sorts of reasons. Often people just decide that they don't like them after a while. Then, the shopkeeper is left with what may be perfectly good used items on his hands and, of course, he wants to sell them again.

Now, some goods are much more likely to be passed off in this way than others. We've noticed that it is common with electrical goods, for example, less so with clothing, toys and so forth. For instance, we recently had a case reported to us where a washing machine was sold as new, but it was actually described in the shop as a 'Manager's Special'. No one thought to ask what that meant, and what it actually meant was that it had been used before and returned for some reason. So, when the new owner called in the repairer, because in fact it didn't work properly, he found someone else's sock inside! Now, that lady had been quite convinced that her machine was new and the shop was later fined four thousand pounds by the court.

So, what advice are we giving to people buying goods of this kind in order for them to avoid getting into this situation in the first place? Firstly, people really need to be aware of what is going on in the shop. Look at how the product is being advertised. Expressions like 'Manager's Special' or 'display model' should warn people to be, at least, suspicious. Ask what it means exactly.

After that there are other things we should be on the look out for. I think, clearly, if some of the documents are missing, which seems to be the case with a lot of these items, the guarantee's not there or there are no instructions, that sort of thing, I think it's reasonable to ask the shop what the situation is, what's happened to it. Another common situation is where the box is obviously not new or possibly damaged in some way and that should ring alarm bells too.

Expressions like 'Manager's Special' don't break the law in themselves, at least not just by saying that, unless they go on to give the impression that the goods are actually new when they are not. So, as that's often the clear impression that people go away with, what we should always do if there's any doubt, is to ask lots of questions. That will put us in the best position to know exactly what we're buying.

[pause]

tone

Now you'll hear Part Two again.

[The recording is repeated.]

[pause]

That's the end of Part Two.
Now turn to Part Three.

PART 3 *You'll hear five people talking about what they did on holiday. For questions 19 to 23, choose from the list of activities A to F which each of them is describing. Use the letters only once. There's one extra letter which you do not need to use.*

You now have thirty seconds in which to look at Part Three.

[pause]

tone

Speaker 1: It was really through college, you see I'd studied this history course and they were organising a tour especially to visit some of the places we'd talked about. My friends thought I was mad, it didn't match their idea of energetic holidays, you know, they were off on mountain adventures and doing watersports but actually, it was quite tiring.

[pause]

Speaker 2: I've always enjoyed being outdoors so hiring a boat for a week seemed the perfect thing to do. Bill wasn't too sure at first – he really wanted to do a bike tour of Scotland, but I promised we'd do that next year. Anyway, once he got used to wind direction and how to steer and things, he really enjoyed it.

[pause]

Speaker 3: I wanted to do something different from lying on the beach and visiting museums. So I booked a few nights in various hotels along the route and we took the train to a starting point. It's very cheap to take your bike on the train. It was hard work at first, all that exercise, my legs really ached but apart from a couple of flat tyres we didn't have any problems.

[pause]

Speaker 4: I went for some practice sessions first. It's very important to get the technique right – body position and using your legs to help you turn. Anyway we had a great time, no accidents, I nearly broke my leg last year when I fell off a horse! This time was fine, the snow conditions were perfect and the lifts weren't too busy. It was wonderful, I'll definitely go again.

[pause]

Speaker 5: The mountains are such a wonderful place to go. Although they're beautiful covered in snow, I prefer them in summer – the scenery is so different. We planned our routes in the evening and set off early every morning. Of course, I made sure I had comfortable boots and that we weren't carrying too much. We kept away from the road and just used the paths, we hardly saw anyone.

[pause]

tone

Now you'll hear Part Three again.

[The recording is repeated.]

[pause]

That's the end of Part Three.
Now turn to Part Four.

PART 4   *You'll hear part of a radio programme about people who become rich quickly. Ann is telling her story. For questions 24 to 30 decide whether the statements are TRUE or FALSE. Write T for True or F for False.*

You now have one minute in which to look at Part Four.

[pause]

tone

Ann: I was brought up in a very ordinary but very happy home with one elder sister, my mother and my father. The great love of my life since I was a small girl was writing, which my family thought was surprising because they didn't consider themselves educated people. I wasn't surprised though because my parents were great readers which is my idea of being educated. Anyway, I trained to be a nurse but whenever I had free time I wrote: poems, short stories, I even once wrote a novel called 'The Pleasure Principle' but I didn't feel comfortable writing longer pieces and I soon went back to my poetry.

Then the strangest thing happened. I had my twenty-first birthday just a few days before and I was feeling very much that I wanted to change things in my life. I'd been nursing a very old woman for several months in a private ward, she told me that although she had lots of relatives, no one came to visit her. Anyway, when she died she left me an enormous sum of money, nearly three-quarters of a million pounds! Of course when the lawyer rang me up and told me I just laughed and thought that my friends were playing a joke on me. So I put down the phone and went in to tell my mother the joke.

But it wasn't a joke! All of a sudden, I was a very rich woman. Well, the first thing was that I was determined that I wouldn't waste the money. Of course I wanted to do something for my family, but all my dad said was 'We're not leaving this house after all the work I've put into the garden!' My mother agreed so all I did was give them something towards a new car and a new greenhouse. My sister was working abroad at this time and when I wrote to tell her the news and offer her some money she said it was *my* money and that she knew I would use it sensibly. None of this really came as a surprise because they've always had a sensible attitude towards money.

But this left me a fortune on my hands to spend! It soon became obvious to me that much as I loved nursing, I loved writing more and that's how I got started. I went to America and did a degree in creative writing. I had a wonderful time and learned a great deal, not from the lecturers necessarily but mainly from other hopeful writers on the course. All this was a decade ago and I've now had several volumes of poetry published. I now want to do something to help other young poets so I'm thinking of setting up a small publishing company which I'll call Grace Park Books after the wonderful old lady who helped me fulfil my life's ambition!

[pause]

tone

Now you'll hear Part Four again.

[The recording is repeated.]

[pause]

That is the end of Part Four.

There'll now be a pause of five minutes for you to copy your answers onto the separate answer sheet. I'll remind you when there is one minute left, so that you're sure to finish in time.

[pause]

You have one more minute left.

[pause]

That's the end of the test. Please stop now. Your supervisor will now collect all the question papers and answer sheets.
Goodbye.

Test 4 Key

Paper 1 Reading (1 hour 15 minutes)

Part 1
1 F   2 H   3 D   4 E   5 G   6 B   7 A

Part 2
8 B   9 B   10 D   11 C   12 A   13 C   14 D

Part 3
15 G   16 E   17 A   18 C   19 D   20 B

Part 4
21 A   22 E   23 H   24/25 E/F *(in any order)*   26/27 B/E *(in any order)*
28 G   29 I   30 C   31 B   32 I   33 G   34/35 F/I *(in any order)*

Paper 2 Writing (1 hour 30 minutes)

Task-specific mark schemes

Question 1

Content
Reply to the friend's letter, accepting the invitation to stay, talking about own preferences and covering the points in the notes: timing; question about the climate; request for advice on clothes to bring; question about the amount of travelling planned. Should convey some enthusiasm/excitement. **NB** Candidate has not been to the country concerned before.

Organisation and cohesion
Clear paragraphing. Opening should refer to original letter and ending look forward to the visit.

Register and format
Informal letter.

Range
Phrases of thanks and enthusiastic acceptance. Language of suggestion. Variety of requests for information. Vocabulary relating to travel/holidays.

Target reader
Would be pleased to hear from the friend and be able to reply to the questions asked.

Question 2 Composition

Content
Composition should give opinions on the topic, giving a balanced argument about the money earned by sports people. **NB** Question could be interpreted as own views or views of the class as a whole.

Range
Phrases to introduce an argument. Language of opinion. Vocabulary relating to money and sport.

Organisation and cohesion
Clear presentation of ideas. Definite conclusion.

Register and format
Neutral, layout of conventional composition.

Target reader
Would be interested and informed.

Question 3 Article

Content
Article should give own and/or friends' views about the importance of clothes and whether there is a connection between what people wear and their personalities.

Range
Phrases to introduce an argument. Language of description. Vocabulary relating to clothes. Adjectives to describe personality.

Organisation and cohesion
Title desirable. Some early attempt to engage the reader, as this is an article. Clear presentation of ideas. Summary conclusion.

Register and format
Consistently informal or neutral.

Target reader
Would be interested and informed.

Question 4 Report

Content
Report should comment on the organisation of the film festival, including both the problems and the successes.

Range
Phrases to introduce positive and negative features. Narrative. Language of evaluation, description and opinion. Vocabulary to do with the cinema/festival events.

Organisation and cohesion
Clear presentation of ideas, though sub-headings not necessary. Definite conclusion.

Register and format
Formal or semi-formal, as suitable for the Club committee.

Target reader
Would be interested and informed.

Question 5 Background reading texts

(a)
Content
Description of the new character. Explanation of how the character could be added to the story and what effect this would have on the story.

Range
Language of description/summarising and explanation.
Possible use of modals.

Organisation and cohesion
Linking of description and explanation.

Appropriacy of register and format
Neutral; composition layout.

Target reader
Would know something about the character to be added, and would understand how the addition of this character would affect the story.

(b)
Content
Description of the cover. Explanation of the cover's significance to the book. An opinion on the extent to which the cover would attract a new reader to the book.

Range
Language of description, explanation and opinion.

Organisation and cohesion
Linking of description, explanation and opinion.

Appropriacy of register and format
Neutral; composition layout.

Target reader
Would have an idea of the book cover and its relevance to the book, and would know whether the writer believes the cover would attract a potential reader to the book.

Paper 3 Use of English (1 hour 15 minutes)

Part 1

1 D	2 C	3 A	4 B	5 A	6 B	7 B	8 C	9 A
10 D	11 A	12 C	13 A	14 D	15 A			

Part 2

16 in/during   17 have   18 known   19 if/whether (*allow*) how
20 spend/take   21 for   22 be   23 what   24 the
25 without   26 or   27 how   28 a   29 yourself   30 and

Part 3

Award one mark for each correct section.
31 if (1) it hadn't/had not been (1)
32 in order (1) to (1)
33 is a (1) waste of (1)
34 not be necessary (1) for you (1)
35 was funnier (1) than my friend (1)
36 cannot read (1) the newspaper without (1)
37 behave (1) so badly that *or* (1) are so badly behaved (1) that (1)
38 was (very) lucky (1) not to (1)
39 anyone (else) anybody/a single person (1) apart from (1)
40 thought (that) Peter (1) was unlikely (1)

Part 4

41 ✓   42 ✓   43 other   44 never   45 years   46 most
47 ✓   48 on   49 ✓   50 too   51 ✓   52 eat   53 time
54 been   55 that

Part 5

56 paintings   57 artist   58 impressive   59 connections
60 surrounding   61 opening   62 unfortunately   63 illness
64 daily   65 admission/admittance

Paper 4 Listening (40 minutes approximately)

Part 1

1 C   2 A   3 C   4 B   5 C   6 B   7 A   8 A

Part 2

9 house   10 the first floor/up a ladder   11 old roses
12 (wonderful) scent(s)/smell(s)   13 mother(-)in(-)law
14 the Children of Riverside   15 drew (the) pictures
16 (the) rooms   17 peace (and quiet)
18 (200) (beautiful) (old) cushion(s)

Part 3

19 E   20 C   21 A   22 F   23 D

Part 4

24 A   25 M   26 S   27 S   28 S   29 M   30 A

Transcript *First Certificate Listening Test. Test Four.*
Hello. I'm going to give you the instructions for this test. I'll introduce each part of the test and give you time to look at the questions. At the start of each piece you'll hear this sound.

tone

You'll hear each piece twice.

Remember, while you're listening, write your answers on the question paper. You'll have time at the end of the test to copy your answers onto the separate answer sheet.

The tape will now be stopped. Please ask any questions now, because you must not speak during the test.

[pause]

PART 1 *Now open your question paper and look at Part One.*
You'll hear people talking in eight different situations. For questions 1 to 8, choose the best answer, A, B or C.

Question 1 *One*
Listen to this man talking to his friend about a meeting. Who turned up at the meeting?
A Marian
B James
C Alison

[pause]

tone

Pete: Hi Marian. What happened to you last night? I thought you were coming to the meeting.
Marian: Was it last night, Pete? Oh, I'm sorry. I completely forgot about it. How did it go?
Pete: Well, it was a bit embarrassing really. There were only two of us. Alison was supposed to be bringing James but he wasn't feeling very well. So she came on her own.
Marian: A bit of a waste of time then?
Pete: Yes – we'd better arrange another meeting on …

[pause]

tone

[The recording is repeated.]

[pause]

Question 2 *Two*
You hear a man complaining about the place where he works. What is the problem in the office?
A the heat
B the noise
C the pollution

[pause]

tone

Man: We have air-conditioning in our office, but because it's not regulated round the floors, on some floors it might be on and on other floors it mightn't be on. It can be quite off-putting. I work on a computer all day, so I've got a fan going all the time which blows all the papers round the room, and the window's open, although we're not supposed to. Because really, in our office, you know, it's quite airless even when it's on.

[pause]

tone

[The recording is repeated.]

[pause]

Question 3   *Three*
You hear somebody talking about choosing a name for something. What is he talking about?
A a children's toy
B a computer game
C a rock band

[pause]

tone

Man: I think the first time I ever really thought about names was when I had to pick one for a group that I'd put together and we picked a terrible name, we called ourselves Buggles. In our heads we saw ourselves as a sort of product from a huge futuristic factory that manufactured compact discs and the Buggles were kind of little robots. It all sounds a bit childish now, doesn't it? If we'd called ourselves something better, well, we might well have sold millions, but when you're called the Buggles, nobody's interested in you.

[pause]

tone

[The recording is repeated.]

[pause]

Question 4   *Four*
You hear somebody talking about the sport of badminton. What point is she making about the sport?
A It's very popular.
B It can be dangerous.
C It's quite exciting.

[pause]

tone

Woman: Forget about skiing and mountain climbing. If you're looking for a sport to inject a little risk into your life, try badminton. For every thousand people who enjoy playing the game in their spare time, thirty-six find themselves laid up with a serious injury according to a recent survey. Nearly half of those were sprains and strains, but knocks and falls were also factors.

[pause]

tone

[The recording is repeated.]

[pause]

Question 5　*Five*
A friend tells you about the time he was robbed. What was his feeling about the incident?
A He felt surprised.
B He felt angry.
C He felt lucky.

[pause]

tone

Man:　People tell me that that's an incredibly safe area but you know I'm never surprised when things go missing from hotel rooms. I mean I would've been really angry if they'd taken my passport and everything but when it's only traveller's cheques I don't think I did too badly.

[pause]

tone

[The recording is repeated.]

[pause]

Question 6　*Six*
You hear the beginning of a radio programme. What is the programme going to be about?
A farming
B baking
C building

[pause]

tone

Radio presenter:　It's a very English scene. A soft summer rain and open countryside as far as the eye can see. I'm in the small village of Batby, on the village green, with a farmer's tractor just behind me, and in front of me the village bakery, a squat, two-storey building built out of local stone, and next to it a pale white house with large windows. And the reason I'm here is because I think that this village probably produces the best bread in the whole of the country, and to prove it there are cars parked all around the little shop that is run by Andy, who I've come to see.

[pause]

tone

[The recording is repeated.]

[pause]

Question 7   *Seven*
Listen to this man talking on the radio. Who is he?
A   an ambulance driver
B   a weatherman
C   a policeman

[pause]

tone

Man: Good evening. I'm very glad to be able to speak to you all this evening. In fact, on the way to the studio, the weather was so bad I didn't think I was going to make it. But this is one thing I want to talk about this evening – getting from one place to another despite the weather. Accidents are often caused by atrocious conditions – snow, ice, freezing fog – and what makes our job difficult is getting to the injured people as quickly as possible so that we can begin treating them. This means that we need training in …

[pause]

tone

[The recording is repeated.]

[pause]

Question 8   *Eight*
Listen to this teacher talking about hiring bicycles. Why is he speaking?
A   to give a warning
B   to change some plans
C   to provide some directions

[pause]

tone

Man: Before you all dash off to hire bicycles for this weekend, you might like to think again! The town is very busy at this time of the year and there's a lot of traffic on the roads. There are a lot of visitors who aren't sure where they're going and are often likely to suddenly change their mind. So, if you do go out, make sure you pay attention at all times.

[pause]

tone

[The recording is repeated.]

[pause]

That's the end of Part One.
Now turn to Part Two.

PART 2   *You'll hear an interview with a woman called Diana Walton at the old house which is her family home. For questions 9 to 18, complete each of the sentences.*

You now have forty-five seconds in which to look at Part Two.

[pause]

tone

Interviewer:	It's a glorious summer's day and I'm looking out over a typical English country garden. I'm at Riverside House and I'm sitting with its owner, Diana Walton. Diana, it's got quite a claim to fame this house, hasn't it?
Diana:	It has indeed. It is the oldest house in Britain that was built as a house, there are some older ones that started off as castles, but this one has always been just a house. It was built in 1130 and much of the original house still remains.
Interviewer:	And which room is this that we're sitting in?
Diana:	Yes, we're now sitting in the hall on the first floor and this was, in fact, the room through which you would have entered the house in 1130, because the front door was then on the first floor, up a ladder which they pulled in after them for safety. And here we are surrounded by the original stone walls, still with the arches.
Interviewer:	And surrounded by this beautiful garden.
Diana:	Yes, it has one of the best collections of old roses in the country, and goes right down to the river. It was laid out by Emily Watson, it was a green field when she came here, but she loved scented plants and certainly everyone who comes here comments on the wonderful smells in the garden.
Interviewer:	You mentioned Emily Watson who is, of course, more famous for her children's books.
Diana:	Yes, she was my mother-in-law in fact, and she first came here when she was fifteen, although it was only at the age of sixty-two that she wrote her first book called, 'The Children of Riverside'. It was based on the house and she wove into the stories descriptions of the house, the gardens and many things in the house itself.
Interviewer:	Which you can still see?
Diana:	Oh yes. Her son Peter actually drew pictures in the book and they're quite faithful to what was described, which is, after all, what is still here.
Interviewer:	And do you get visits from fans of the books?
Diana:	Certainly. It's absolutely magical for readers of the books to be able to come and walk into the world they've read about. There's always a gasp of pleasure when people walk in and recognise the rooms described in the books.
Interviewer:	Do you get many visitors?
Diana:	Yes, we're open to the public on summer Saturdays and people come to see the house and gardens. The house always gives people enormous pleasure whether or not they know the books because it has such a feeling of peace and quiet.
Interviewer:	Mmm, it certainly does. And also on the sofa here are some of the many beautiful old cushions that seem to be everywhere.
Diana:	That's right. Emily Watson made a collection of over two hundred old cushions, many of them made in this house over the centuries and they're becoming very well known internationally and some visitors come because they know there's such an important collection here.
Interviewer:	Diana, thank you so much for letting us visit your house today.
Diana:	It's been my pleasure.

[pause]

tone

Now you'll hear Part Two again.

[The recording is repeated.]

[pause]

That's the end of Part Two.
Now turn to Part Three.

PART 3   *You'll hear five different men talking about silence. For questions 19 to 23, choose from the list A to F who is speaking. Use the letters only once. There is one extra letter which you do not need to use.*

You now have thirty seconds in which to look at Part Three.

[pause]

tone

Speaker 1:   Silences can be worrying because the fear arises in your listeners that something has gone wrong. What every broadcaster is taught to avoid is dead air. Dead air is something which bores, whereas a meaningful silence is important. Without a certain amount of silence, broadcasting would be terribly unrelaxing. But the big fear is, you know, especially on the late night show, you put on a song and you pop out to go to the bathroom or for a sandwich and you don't quite get back in time.

[pause]

Speaker 2:   To get to the heart of a piece you have to discover its breathing-in moments, the listening moments. When you're on stage and not speaking, you have to teach yourself to stay in the role, and you have to look natural; and to do that you have to think of all the reasons why you are not speaking at that moment. Then when your line comes, you have to feel very desperate to speak at that moment. If not, why were you silent for so long?

[pause]

Speaker 3:   We definitely set out to make witnesses nervous by remaining silent in the hope that the person will go on to say something which is particularly useful to us. There is a type of silence which is important and which is normally controlled by the professionals in court because they know what they're doing, and they've been taught to keep silent, so that the other person will carry on speaking, will fill the gap. So, if you ever have to go to court, it's essential to learn that when you've finished speaking, you shut up!

[pause]

Speaker 4:   All my training makes me want to get someone talking and keep them talking, to fill the space, to make them finish. But actually silence is essential to a human voice telling you something interesting. It may mean your guest is hiding something, or sometimes waiting to decide whether to say something in front of the camera. So, there's the silence that you leave because something interesting may be coming, and there's the silence that you wait for because people sometimes repeat things to give them emphasis, or change things slightly.

[pause]

Speaker 5: For me, it's a question of concentration. When I'm on court, I need to think very carefully about what I'm doing. People think it's all physical strength and speed, but to play well you actually have to think it through, plan your next shot, get your opponent on the wrong foot. So when someone in the crowd laughs or coughs and breaks my concentration, I get really mad. But you can't show that, it's a lesson in self control, in learning not to be put off by things.

[pause]

tone

Now you'll hear Part Three again.

[The recording is repeated.]

[pause]

That's the end of Part Three.
Now turn to Part Four.

PART 4 *You'll hear a conversation between three people who are organising a sports day in their village. For questions 24 to 30, write S for Susan, A for Alan or M for Marie.*

You now have forty-five seconds in which to look at Part Four.

[pause]

tone

Susan: Right, let's get started shall we? Thanks for coming Alan and Marie, I know how busy you both are. Now, we decided at the last meeting that the basic programme would be a sports day with a disco later in the evening.

Alan: I've been thinking Susan, we need to get someone interesting to open the event, don't we? You know, make a speech.

Susan: Yes, I was just coming to that, any ideas?

Alan: Well, there's a chap at my running club who's just been in an International competition. We could ask him.

Marie: That sounds good. I couldn't come up with anyone.

Susan: Decided then, make a note of that Alan. Now the next item is the children's games. We need someone to be in charge of them in the day. Marie?

Marie: I'll do that if you like. I'm sure I'll enjoy running the competitions.

Susan: It'll be hard work – I know, I've done it before. Now, if I were you Marie, I'd make sure I had plenty of helpers and don't let that Mick Brown get involved or he'll take over.

Marie: I'll remember that Susan. What about the hall, for the evening do?

Alan: We have a problem there. Mr Taylor says it's not available that evening, something to do with it being repainted, he's worried about the paint getting marked.

Susan: Nonsense, he's just making excuses. Go and see him again and insist we need it that evening.

Alan: OK. By the way Susan, did you find out about that disco you mentioned?

Susan: Oh no, I completely forgot. Sorry, look I'll definitely do that tomorrow and let you both know immediately.

Marie: We need to make a decision about the food too.
Susan: Yes, that's next on my agenda. Now I think we should have a hot meal. That would be nice, there are plenty of tables and chairs for everyone.
Marie: I don't think that's practical. You'd just make more work for everyone. A few sandwiches is much easier.
Susan: I suppose you're right. Put that down Alan. Did anyone remember to ask about getting the invitations printed?
Marie: I couldn't get through on the phone.
Susan: Alan?

Alan: I got a rough estimate for the cost. The printer says if we let him have the exact details, he'll give us a price.
Susan: Well done, that's about it for tonight. If we meet again on Friday, we can finalise all the details.

[pause]

tone

Now you'll hear Part Four again.

[The recording is repeated.]

[pause]

That is the end of Part Four.

There'll now be a pause of five minutes for you to copy your answers onto the separate answer sheet. I'll remind you when there's one minute left, so that you're sure to finish in time.

[pause]

You have one more minute left.

[pause]

That's the end of the test. Please stop now. Your supervisor will now collect all the question papers and answer sheets.
Goodbye.